AMADEUS

OTHER PLAYS BY PETER SHAFFER

Peter Shaffer's

AMADEUS

A PLAY

WITH AN INTRODUCTION BY
THE DIRECTOR SIR PETER HALL

~ AND ~

A WHOLLY NEW PREFACE
BY THE AUTHOR

HARPER  PERENNIAL

NEW YORK • LONDON • TORONTO • SYDNEY

This work was first published in England in 1980 by André Deutsch Limited, in somewhat different form.

The first U.S. edition of this book was published in 1981 by Harper & Row, Publishers, in somewhat different form.

First Perennial Library edition published 1981.
First Perennial edition published 2001.

Designed by The Book Design Group

Library of Congress Cataloging-in-Publication Data is available.
ISBN 0-06-093549-9

15 16   WB/RRD   30 29 28 27 26 25

For

Robert

with undying love

I would like to give special thanks to the excellent and long-suffering original publisher of this play, Michael Bessie. Mike oversaw the last publication of *Amadeus* by Harper & Row in 1981, and among all the other masters of their craft mentioned in my preface he most particularly deserves to be greeted here, with fond and grateful salutation.

P.S.

INTRODUCTION
BY SIR PETER HALL

I want to write about the 1998–99 revival of *Amadeus* in London and New York, and about how the text, presented here, is to my mind the culmination of more than twenty years of work.

Lightning, they say (and they say it with particular foreboding on Broadway), is not known to strike in the same place twice. Some twenty years ago, *Amadeus* bestowed Tonys on me, on Peter Shaffer, Ian McKellen and John Bury, the designer. It was an undoubted hit and ran for almost three years. Why on earth, my friends nervously inquired, did I want to direct it again in 1998? And it was not even to be the same production. I was bent on different designs, a different cast, and the production had a much older writer and director. Most of all, there was a possibility to reconsider the text.

Revivals of ancient successes, particularly musicals, are something of a tradition on Broadway and in London. But they are usually (particularly on Broadway) akin to the original productions, dusted down in a spirit of loving nostalgia. To do a new production of an old hit might seem to cast doubt on its original validity. Broadway is a superstitious place: it hates meddling with legends.

So that was the risk. *Amadeus* is probably the most successful serious play of the last half century. It has triumphed everywhere. So what is its extraordinary appeal? Why would it be exciting to direct again? And why did Peter Shaffer want to continue rewriting it?

Amadeus is a clear-eyed celebration of Mozart and his music. He is someone whose genius can stand with Shakespeare's. Wolfgang is of course dangerous to let onto the stage, because playwright and actors have to live up to a creativity that is almost superhuman. He also happens to be one of the great theater composers: his music easily commands a stage. But if the portrait can be convincing, the fascination is boundless—and makes for high drama.

Shaffer's play of course goes deeper. It looks unblinkingly at the rest of us, who are neither blessed nor cursed (like Mozart) with genius. It analyzes with compassion and wit how desperately ordinary most of us are. For however talented we may secretly think ourselves to be, we remain in the great scheme of things relative mediocrities. It is only genius—that rarest and most precious of states—that is unaffected by fashion and indifferent to competition. Only genius goes on creating, whatever the circumstances; it needs neither success nor recognition to sustain it: van Gogh never sold a painting. Only genius makes its own rules.

And we desperately need genius. With the decline of religious faith, artists become more and more our spiritual guides. We urgently scan the past, hoping for some clues for the future. Hence our modern passion for biography: sometimes, indeed, we appear more interested in the artist than in the art. We need to believe that a good artist is also a good man, and we learn time and time again, but never remember, that this is a naïve assumption. Wagner was a deeply horrible man, yet that does not diminish the virtue and vitality of his music. "Goodness is nothing in the furnace of art," says Shaffer's Salieri, the mediocrity who recognizes in Mozart's music the voice of God.

The play asks why God would seem to bestow genius so indiscriminately, indifferent to morality or human decency. Salieri worships Mozart's music yet is consumed by a jealous hatred of the selfish creature who creates it. Salieri is seen as the balanced man of the Enlightenment, virtuous, Catholic—and, in his music, a man of classical discipline, affronted by Mozart's artful dissonances and sudden painful chromaticisms. Yet he is also overwhelmed by Mozart's originality. As influential Court Composer, he can advance Mozart's career and prosperity. Instead he withholds his patronage. The play (and history) does not say that Salieri killed Mozart. But by blocking his advancement at court in a thousand covert ways he makes it impossible for Mozart to live. And by destroying him, he destroys himself, and the genius that the musician in him worships.

Of course the play is drama, not fact, although the majority of its scenes are based on a nugget of historical truth. One obviously is not: the great Act Two confrontation between the two men which probably never happened in any form, and if it did we are only able to guess at what was said. But this invented scene allows Shaffer to show the heart of his play. Significantly, it is the scene that has undergone the most revision over the twenty years of the play's existence. The dramatist has not been altering, but revealing. Now I think he has found it.

All Shaffer's major plays are about the quest for God: if He exists, why is He so uncaring? So the final contest in *Amadeus* is not between Salieri and Mozart but between Salieri and God. God *allows* Mozart to exist; indeed, He uses him. Salieri in contrast finds himself facing a selfish and uncaring God, who follows His own incomprehensible needs and is indifferent to the suffering of Man. He is indeed so elusive that His very existence has to be questioned. And if He exists, why did He create the world and then seemingly walk away from it, leaving mediocre Man to suffer in confusion?

When Peter Shaffer and the producer, Kim Poster, asked me to do the play again, my first reaction was to refuse. I had lived through half a dozen casts, from Paul Scofield to Ian McKellen; and there had been productions all over the world (the original Broadway production has just been revived for the umpteenth time in Japan). I thought I would be in danger of repeating myself.

Then I remembered, with a flood of pleasure, how Peter Shaffer works and what a joy it is to share the process with him. He has never finished with a play: each production presents a fresh opportunity to challenge the validity of the material. Sometimes there are little adjustments, sometimes whole scenes. In December 1981 we opened on Broadway with a second act entirely different from the one we had performed at the National Theatre in London the year before. It was more human and more tragic. This process—a journey from admittedly thrilling melodrama to a full humanist tragedy—has continued. And the extraordinary thing about this work—which Shaffer calls "carving a play with actors"—is that in my experience the rewrites are always improvements: they get nearer and nearer to the heart of the play.

To my surprise, rereading it excited me profoundly. It was more a tragedy than I had remembered: an agony of bewildered pain rather than an exciting thriller. I realized that Shaffer's continual work had increased the dimensions of the play. And, to excite me further, there was the prospect of collaborating with David Suchet—a tragic actor of the first rank, whom I had always extravagantly admired but had never worked with. A phone call with Shaffer confirmed that he wanted to do still more work. It began to look promising.

We opened at the Old Vic in London in 1998. We then came to the Ahmanson Theatre in October 1999 to begin our pre-Broadway tour. There should be a plaque on the wall of that theater— "*Amadeus* was finished here October 1999 after twenty years of work"—because the text-work continued there and was (I think) finally concluded.

Scholars will have a merry time with the text of *Amadeus* in the future: there are so many versions—even published ones. They will be able to worry and fret over the differences well into this century. Shaffer has been like a sculptor chipping away at the block of marble, working carefully to release the figure that is concealed within its depths. The play I originally directed at the National Theatre had all the thrills of a melodrama by E. T. A. Hoffmann. In New York, in the 1980s, the play became an anguished metaphysical debate as well. Now, after twenty years, while keeping its thrills and its intellectual edge, it has become a profoundly humanist play about forgiveness and atonement. It is extraordinary that after twenty years a dramatist can work with such passion. He is not trying to find what he means: he knows that. Say rather he is trying to define his meaning more completely in the white heat of the theater.

I have revisited many plays, but none with more pleasure than *Amadeus*. I've done three *Godot*s, two *Homecoming*s, two *Cymbeline*s, four *Dream*s, three *Hamlet*s and half a dozen *Figaro*s. Sometimes they have been reworkings of an original production; sometimes they have been completely new propositions, with new designs. It depends on the time, the place and the cast. A director's job is as subjective and instinctive as an actor's: he can only trust himself. But he must try to communicate the heart of the play to his particular audience, and the more he knows about a great piece, the better his work will be. Sometimes I think I would like to be a conductor, if I ever get the chance of reincarnation. They perform a piece many times.

Past directorial work can never revive precisely, because such a revival would involve an imposition of old solutions on new circumstances: it is not creative. It may, however, be a legitimate starting point. I tried in 1990 to do a new production of Pinter's *Homecoming*. But the original 1965 production, with John Bury's masterly set, kept surging through my head. So the set had to be the beginning of the new production. To impose something else would have been self-conscious. *Amadeus* presented a different set of problems. I found I couldn't remember—twenty years on—very much about the original production. To try to do it again would be not a revival but an exhumation. I remembered the music—not only each piece but exactly where it began and ended. But then I have always had a better memory for music than for words or pictures.

John Bury's beautiful original designs were based on Baroque theater. Salieri was "performing" his life for the audience. Now, it seemed to me, I wanted to go a step further. The play was a performance of his memories, opulent certainly, but able to change with the speed of light. I had my beginning: the changing images of memory. I said I would do the production.

Peter Shaffer's *Amadeus* has always roused high passions: it has its finger on a spot that many find uncomfortable. That, I suspect, is why it has always been so commercial. Nonetheless, there have always been those who cannot bear the destruction of the delicate porcelain Mozart—the composer of tinkling elegance—and the revelation of the mortal child that we meet in his letters.

Margaret Thatcher was not known for her enthusiasm for the arts. She visited the National Theatre only once during my fifteen years as its director. Unfortunately, it was to see *Amadeus*. She was not pleased. In her best headmistress style, she gave me a severe wigging for putting on a play that depicted Mozart as a scatological imp with a love of four-letter words. It was inconceivable, she said, that a man who wrote such exquisite and elegant music could be so foulmouthed. I said that Mozart's letters proved he was just that: he had an extraordinarily infantile sense of humor. In a sense, he protected himself from maturity by indulging his childishness.

"I don't think you heard what I said," replied the Prime Minister. "He couldn't have been like that."

I offered (and sent) a copy of Mozart's letters to Number Ten the next day. I was even thanked by the appropriate Private Secretary. But it was useless: the Prime Minister insisted that I was wrong, so wrong I was.

With the play and then the film, I would think that Peter Shaffer has done more to encourage the love and understanding of Mozart than anyone this century. I was glad to be alongside him again, undertaking this new journey. It was a new cast, new sets and, as far as I was concerned, a new play. I started again.

When I am preparing a production, I scribble notes to myself in a little book. They are reminders, quotations, problems, tentative solutions. Often, I find the same solutions written down three or four times—always as if they were new discoveries. I am not therefore saying that a comparison with the original ghostly prompt copy wouldn't sometimes reveal the same solution for a scene. It is just that I genuinely don't remember them. We often end where we began. But Peter Shaffer is the exception: he begins all over again in all humility. And here, to my mind, he has brilliantly uncovered what he meant.

PREFACE
AMADEUS: THE FINAL ENCOUNTER
BY PETER SHAFFER

The Scene of the last meeting in my play between Salieri and Mozart was always hard for me to get right.

Structurally it obviously forms the climax of the piece. The whole impetus of its story increasingly demands a final confrontation of some kind between those two desperate men: some dramatic resolution, even if it has to be fashioned out of the impediment of a situation that can never really be resolved.

The historical facts are not helpful; they are even in some ways anticlimactic. Salieri survived Mozart by thirty-four years, living on in Vienna, at first in his accustomed state of huge fame and honor until—inevitably in that superficial and impatient town—it faded away completely. The First Imperial Kappellmeister lingered on in ever-increasing obscurity, a new tide of Romanticism running in to obliterate his Classicism, popular taste for musical easiness relentlessly overwhelming the virtually used-up formulae of his restrained compositional language. He abandoned writing opera, at which he had most succeeded; his audience turned to less austere and more sugary forms of it; and finally he came to find himself a ghost—retired, replaced and essentially rejected.

Then suddenly, at the age of seventy-three, no doubt abetted by this wounding experience, there came an act of terrible violence. The old man attempted to cut his throat and spent his last three

years in the City Infirmary, endlessly accusing himself of having
poisoned his immortal rival to death. Between 1823 and 1825
these anguished declarations were duly reported in respectable
newspapers and periodicals, and they also appear in the Conversation Books of Beethoven, where visiting friends wrote down the
news for the deaf man. These are quoted verbatim to the theater
audience in the last moments of *Amadeus*.

Unquestionably these convulsed self-denunciations form together the smoke that proverbially indicates fire: they stink of
burning guilt, and fearful desolation. But, unfortunately for the
dramatist, none of them contains the slightest suggestion of a serious emotional confrontation having occurred between himself and
Mozart. Of course this is hardly surprising, since it is the nature of
professional assassination to be covert. Nevertheless, for the purposes of Drama, there *needs* to be such a Scene: the play urgently
demands one. Just as Schiller's Queen of Scots must face his Queen
of England brow to brow, so must my protagonists confront each
other. Something—admission or denial, shame or justification,
defiance or repentance—has to be revealed to Salieri's victim, and
whatever transpires at the conclusion of it has to tighten even more
sharply the vise of his torment. Paradoxically, the scene must
simultaneously release its audience through a sense of Form and
increase the irremovable anguish of its Narrator. The objection
that no evidence exists for such encounter is no excuse for not pro-
viding one. The playwright's absolute obligations are clear: to
obey the formal insistences of theater, employing Possibility and
Credibility as his counselors, and proudly to produce the specific
electricity which he may thereby be able to conjure.

My task here is to review the half dozen Versions of the climax,
which I constructed over twenty years under this hard imperative.
Thankfully, in doing so, I had the unflagging support of my singu-
larly patient and sympathetic director, Peter Hall, who actually
staged the play twice (and brilliantly) in entirely different productions of 1979 and 1999; also the enthusiastic cooperation of Milos

Forman, who filmed it in 1982, and the loving assistance of several
finely intelligent actors along the way.

However, in the end, of course, the whole conceptual struggle
remained what all such writing has to be: the rigorous, obsessed
and solitary exercise of the Author. I recall it here now, as briefly as
I can, so that this book may stand as at least the partial record of a
compulsive and long-evolving process.

THE FIRST VERSION OF THE LAST ENCOUNTER

Amadeus was presented by the National Theatre of Great Britain
in December 1979 with Paul Scofield as Salieri and Simon Callow
as Mozart. It was a tremendous success with the public; the Sunday *Times* of London reported that people were lining up outside
the theater at six-thirty each morning for seats available only that
day. I mention this agreeable fact only to make it clear that it was
not because the play was a failure that I became involved in changing it. From the start of its run I was aware of a certain dissatisfac-
tion in myself with its second act. For one thing, Salieri had not
enough to do *histrionically* with making Mozart's ruin. He was a
little too removed from it, insufficiently contributing to the action
through other people, and not quite where he should have been—
at the wicked center of it all. This was particularly noticeable with
regard to the circumstances surrounding the commissioning of the
Requiem, which had to lead directly to whatever climax was
involved.

The factual truth of this anonymous commission is almost too
improbable for belief. On a morning in the autumn of 1791, as
Mozart sat working alone in his poor lodging in the Rauhensteingasse, the figure of a man, extremely tall and cadaverous, all muffled in grey and staring out at the world with the face of a
death's-head, entered unannounced. In deep sepulchral tones he

declared: "I am sent by my Master to commission from you a Requiem Mass." Mozart naturally asked: "Who is this Master? And who has died?" The reply came: "Do not seek to know. Only work fast. He will be much displeased if the work is not finished when you see me next." Then he set down a modest bag of money, turned and left the room. The distraught composer, in rotten health and now living largely on medicines and cheap white wine—also quite alone since his wife had (temporarily) abandoned him—at once conceived the vile idea that the Figure was a visitant from the other world, ordering him to compose the Mass for his own death.

In actuality, this Messenger was simply an exceptionally tall, skeletal fellow named Leutgeb, the grim-looking Steward of a rich and eccentric music lover called Count Walsegg, who actually maintained a private orchestra and was consumed by a desperate desire to be regarded as a composer. The Count's wife had just died, so he sent this alarming servant anonymously to Mozart in strictest secrecy to commission her Requiem. Incredibly, his plan was simply to copy out the manuscript in his own hand, perform it in his mansion before an audience of friends—and pass it off as his own work!

In the first production of the play, I employed this weird true story as part of the mechanism of the plot to lead the action to its climax. I invented for Salieri a cadaverous and fanatically religious Valet whom I called Greybig. Salieri confessed to the audience that he had somehow learnt of the Count's preposterous intention and offered to help him accomplish it; accordingly he dispatched his own Valet, in grey cloak and mask, to commission the Requiem from Mozart, in secret and anonymously. He informed Greybig that Mozart was a libertine composer of sublime talent, who had written no religious music for years, that he was rotten with sexual disease and might soon die, and that for the good of his soul he must be persuaded into writing the great Church Mass he was put on earth to compose. The Valet must order him to begin immediately, and finish without delay. Salieri's real motive in doing this, as he also confessed to us, was "a design to hasten Mozart toward madness, or toward death."

In other words, Salieri took a backseat whilst his servant did the dirty work, on and off stage, until one day the man flatly refused to go on with it. It was only then that his master excitedly took over *himself*, donning the same cloak and mask and appearing nightly below Mozart's window, extending his fingers upwards and implacably reducing their number with each visit to indicate the days running out for the terrified creature writing frantically above. Finally, when there was none left to show, the crazed Kapellmeister wickedly changed his gestures into a slow and insistent *beckoning*. Whereupon, half in terror, half in bravado, Mozart threw open his casement and called down to him, using the words of Leporello from his opera *Don Giovanni*, inviting the statue to dinner: *"O statua gentilissima, venite a cena!"* And so began the First Version of the Last Encounter, with Salieri unable to help himself, accepting the invitation—"tramping up the stairs with stone feet," and entering the miserable chamber of his now demented rival.

This confrontation scene, bravely played by Scofield and Callow, was quite short. It involved a scared, disordered speech from Mozart, drunkenly apologetic for not having finished the Mass, confessing a feeling of being poisoned, and imploring more time, the while desperately hugging Salieri's knees until finally the man could bear it no longer and, with a great shout of self-loathing, tore off the mask and revealed himself. There followed a dreadful silence—and then suddenly Mozart's shrill accusation that his "friend" had murdered him. *And, helplessly, Salieri admitted it!*

In a reply consisting only of the word *yes*, repeated ten times, he acknowledged the truth of the accusation: *"Eccomi!—il tuo assassino! . . . For you I go to Hell."* And in answer to Wolfgang's horrified, uncomprehending "Why's?," he added: *"Eccomi—il tua vittima! . . . Be with God!"* Then gravely he bowed to the swaying

Mozart and departed. As Mozart fell, calling out for his wife and crawling weakly over the floor to his worktable, Salieri walked downstage and addressed the audience:

> And there it was. It came out of me so easily, the appalling lie! . . . Why? Because it was true. I *had* poisoned him. Not with arsenic. No. With everything you've seen me do.

Then Mozart painfully clambered up the table and turned it thereby into his deathbed, curling up on a mattress made of uncompleted manuscripts of the Requiem. Salieri continued:

> Oh, my friends: when you come here, you will feel! God cannot feel. He can only need. He cannot pity. Only Man can pity. Only Man can know shame. Only Man can *atone*. [*Pause*] In that freezing slum I saw my victim. I stood there in my masquerade and looked on my work. The slashes I had cut in him, the Creature. The stinking wounds of all hope denied him. I saw the kind of murderer I was. And I confessed.

And the Scene finished thus:

SALIERI: I knew he would repeat it through the City.
MOZART: *Salieri!* . . .
SALIERI: And the city would repeat it through the world.
MOZART: Salieri! . . .
SALIERI: And the world through the years after he died—as die he must—louder and louder. As his fame grew, so would mine. "Salieri, the poisoner of Mozart!" Just that. A horror for all eternity. *Bene e bene ancora!* This would be my atonement!

THE SECOND VERSION

In some ways the above Scene (to be found only in the first version of the play, published in London by André Deutsch in 1980, with a glorious photograph on the cover of Scofield as the shawled and dressing-gowned old monster) was tremendously effective. It allowed both actors to play with all guns of melodrama blazing, but, more important, it contained the idea of Salieri's increasing need for *atonement*—a theme which was abandoned in the succeeding Version brilliantly acted on Broadway with Ian McKellen (and then all over the world by many other actors) and only put back much later, when I came to work on the play again with David Suchet twenty years after. I stress this most particularly because what in 1999 was announced as a wholly new—and, in some criticisms, misguided rewrite—really contained at its heart a motif which had actually been there from the beginning. I had dropped it, largely I think because I had come to feel that a lust for repentance might be a weakening emotion in Salieri's strongly villainous character. Now I believe I was wrong. "A small-town Catholic, full of dread," as he came to define himself, would almost certainly become invaded by a deep measure of guilt, especially when confronted by the now helpless and dying object of his hitherto pitiless persecution.

Incidentally, the need for atonement also gave to this First Version another and most powerful dimension to the whispers that open the play. It was originally Salieri's idea to circulate the calumny through gossiping Vienna that he was a factual—not just a metaphorical—murderer, as an extravagant act of *penance*, violently besmirching his own reputation forever. In all later versions the same idea is replaced by another, far less worthy motive: to grab a piece of Mozart's immortality at any price, so that he would live for future generations, "if not in fame, at least in infamy!" I did this because I felt that the figure we see thirty-odd years later should be more recognizably *unbalanced*—even in defeat still challenging God. The effect of the rewrite is to substitute a blackly comic effect for a tragic one. (The line about his becoming immortal after all is always greeted with a huge laugh in the theater—as is the moment when his suicide attempt is unsuccessful and his batty intention thwarted.) All the same, over the years, I really came to think it had been an error to dispense with the theme of atonement so completely.

Why, it may be asked, did I actually embark on the long process of changing *anything?* The answer is threefold, and entirely to do with the commissioning of the Requiem. (A) Salieri's action in dispatching his Valet to Mozart was a wrong choice because it was highly improbable that he would ever get to hear about Count Walsegg's extremely secret plan to pass it off as his own work in the first place. (B) Sending his Valet was far too public an act for Salieri to initiate; he was much too oblique and hidden a plotter to risk being connected with it, or having his servant gossip about it later to others. (C) I came to realize that there was no way at all that Salieri could reckon on Mozart behaving in the weirdly superstitious manner we now know that he did when confronted with the real-life Steward of Count Walsegg—treating him as a Messenger from the Other World. This was to read History backwards. My whole invention in fact was a rather too cheeky exercise in hindsight.

Clearly I had to devise a more natural way into my climactic Last Encounter. Salieri's complicity with Walsegg had to go, and so did Salieri's complicitous Valet. Although he had been played at the Olivier Theatre with a splendid spookiness by the actor Philip Locke, I reluctantly exercised the dramatist's divine right of character assassination and killed off Greybig. Now, whatever I devised, Salieri would have to move to the center in this part of the play, as I had long wished him to do.

The solution lay finally in inventing something that somehow foreshadowed the arrival of the real Grey Messenger sent by Walsegg, an incident too dramatic in its horrid influence over

Mozart's imaginings for me not to use. I decided therefore to invent for him a recurring *dream,* containing a menacing image prefiguring the Count's grim Steward: a misty Figure cloaked and faceless, but with extended arms approaching nearer every night. That gesture was suggested by the sinister beckoning of Scofield in the First Version—an image both paternal and eternal, and growing more urgent with each visitation.

Let me say that this was not just a contrivance. I was sure it was an entirely natural and credible dream for Wolfgang to have, considering the guilt he almost surely must have felt heavily after the death of the father he had regarded all his life as his only real Protector, but whom he had neglected markedly in the aging man's last years, spent all alone miles away in Salzburg. And of course such a menacing dream was also informed by my knowledge of what he was going to tell Salieri in their final meeting: that he is writing the music for his own death.

Having created the dream, and of course getting Mozart to tell it to his increasingly trusted new friend, I was able to expand the whole notion of Salieri offering himself as a substitute father. This theme became extremely explicit in the new Version. It remained only for Mozart to run to him in terror, announcing that the Grey Figure in his dream had actually become *real*—acquiring a skull for a face and boldly invading his apartment to demand a Requiem—and the scene was set for Salieri to conceive the cruelest thing he could do to his victim. He would appear *himself* before him, disguised as the Messenger. In his view, of course, Mozart was now starting to "see things": an opinion shared by the audience—who were only told in an aside after his death that the incident with the skeletal figure coming into his chamber had not been a hallucination at all but a real event.

What all this led to was a significant transformation of the Confrontation Scene, achieved on the pre-Broadway tour in Washington. The first great change occurred with the introduction of the actual music of the Requiem. As soon as Salieri reluctantly received a page of the opening movement at the hands of the sick Mozart and sat, still masked, to read it, something glorious happened. As soon as one heard that grief-drenched sound of the Kyrie staining the atmosphere with its aching D Minor lamentation, whilst over it Mozart spoke his own *verbal* lament for his spent youth, the temperature rose perceptively. Since the first time I heard it in rehearsal, standing in the stalls of the theater, that moment has always been unnervingly moving to me. Suddenly we were in a world totally different from the First Version.

The ensuing week was a tremendously difficult time of labor for the four of us: two magnificently unflagging actors, a director with nerves of steel and a stubbornly possessed author. Together at full stretch over five feverish days, we worked out a largely new Last Encounter. I would write a virtually fresh version of the Scene every morning and leave it at the desk of the Guest Quarters Hotel for Ian McKellen and Tim Curry; they would learn it in the afternoon; Peter Hall would direct it in the early evening, and they would play it as convincingly as they could (which meant very) two hours later before an audience, for us to evaluate. We were all simultaneously wrecked and exhilarated by the challenge of breakneck discovery.

At one performance I conceived the most extreme innovation—Salieri actually *eating* a piece of the paper on which the Kyrie is written, to demonstrate his own poison, and spitting it out at its composer. At another, one of the most effective moments found by Hall was the gentle removal of Salieri's mask by Mozart standing *behind* him as he sat. And, finally, the Scene ended with Wolfgang scuttling under a long worktable, desperately singing his father's little bedtime "Kissing Song" to the tune of "Twinkle, Twinkle, Little Star," with Salieri yelling down through it from above, "Alone! Leave me alone, *ti imploro!* Leave me alone at last!"

The entire sequence worked extremely well on the tingling plane of melodrama—although I confess it finally went too far, with Mozart imagining he saw his father in the room, and trying

to leap up into his arms to form an ending which, despite its bold-
ness, always somewhat embarrassed me. In sum, however, I was
pleased with our joint labors, although still not entirely satisfied.
The Scene really demanded something more searching than fireworks.

I was going to have to wait quite a long time before I at last
saw on stage a version which pleased me all through.

THE THIRD VERSION

The film of *Amadeus* was vastly different from the play, and its
treatment of the elusive Final Encounter was spectacularly so:
utterly improbable, and in many ways entirely fitting!

Obviously the Broadway rewrite was much too "theatrical"
for the screen, and once more finding a substitute taxed ingenuity
to the full. Milos Forman and I holed up in his Connecticut farm-
house for what seemed years (actually about sixteen weeks) and
came up in the end with a script which was filmed virtually without alteration of any kind in Prague in 1983. Privately I mourned
the frequently banal simplification of the language but became
partly persuaded that it was, for movie purposes, unavoidable.

Its astonishing triumph worldwide ensured that more people
actually received and rejoiced in Mozart's music in one year than
in all the nearly two hundred years since his death. As with Shakespeare, even such potentially annihilating popularity—the tapes of
our sound track (designed by myself) misused in apparently every
café on earth—could not stale the eternal miracle of his sound.
And unquestionably the solution we found for the final encounter
was in part responsible for that success, ensuring that there was a
highly appropriate dramatic climax to crown the film and excite its
viewers.

This solution was actually conceived out of a sudden realization that the logic of the story could well lead finally to a desperate attempt by the obsessed and increasingly unbalanced Salieri actually to *steal* the Requiem Mass he knows Mozart is writing, and then pass it off as his own work: a grieving Tribute offered at his rival's tragic funeral, which might not be far off. The idea of course was obviously suggested to me by the equally unlikely but true tale of Count Walsegg's secret commission. However, it also obviously inferred the possible necessity of having actually to murder Mozart—which for me was always a coarse and unacceptable finale. Only when the much less sensational idea arrived of an extremely sick Mozart collapsing at a performance of *The Magic Flute* and being borne off by Salieri to a sickbed, which would prove his deathbed, did things come together.

The piece of music I selected from the Requiem to be dictated by the dying Mozart to a ravening Salieri was the opening of the Confutatis. I actually traveled out to Minneapolis to see the music director of our film, Sir Neville Marriner, and persuaded him to lie on a sofa and perform the part of an expiring young genius, urgently dictating that movement whilst I sat beside him, pen in trembling hand, playing an eager and predatory Salieri. As I recall it, my verbal part consisted largely of crying, "Not so fast!" over and over again.

It was a bold but right decision to construct this Scene deliberately as the climax, because its central preoccupation is exclusively with *sound*—and Sound is actually the name of the main character in our story. Neither of the principal human characters moves much: one lies on his soaked mattress sweating to compose in his head, the other sits at the foot of it, sweating with greed as he scribbles it all down for his own despicable uses. On paper it all looks to be pretty uncinematic—just line after line of instrumental and vocal notation—but when it is played on a screen, it bursts into vibrant life.

I was especially pleased because I had reflected as I wrote that it would really be an excellent achievement if I could demonstrate, even in a rather obvious way, the kind of mental effort this unique genius could engage in. It involved conjuring almost instantaneously out of his head long aural sequences, heard by him both individually and interlocking, to make a perfectly formed and (in both senses) perfectly moving sound. If the resulting music had not been good, the process would have been no more than a curious phenomenon. But here what was written was actually the code for a profound and absolute beauty, simultaneously fixed in structure, intensity, key and color, all in the same working minute. And I wanted viewers, especially younger ones, who sometimes tend to imagine the act of composition more or less as simply croaking tentatively to a guitar, to feel something of the awe—though not of course the envy—my Salieri knew.

The only thing I regretted about this Scene was actually a dialogue improvisation exchanged by the two actors in the heat of shooting, when Salieri failed to follow Mozart's direction that the drums "go with the harmony." It really would be very unlikely indeed for him not to be able to understand a statement so obviously basic, and, as Mozart has already pointed out, Salieri's own music is largely made of such obviousness.

THE FOURTH VERSION

After the film, the first significant new stage production of *Amadeus* with which I was again involved was in 1997 at the Stratford Festival Theatre, Ontario. It was very beautifully set by Desmond Healey and boasted a fine performance of Salieri by Brian Bedford, a dedicated and hugely accomplished actor who, over the years, has excellently played several of my other pieces, starting with *Five Finger Exercise* and including *Equus*. For him, I renewed my struggle with the Last Encounter. For a moment I was tempted to try putting the bedroom dictation scene from the film onto the stage, but I soon came to feel that it would not work. Paradoxically I felt that the very quality I cherished about it on the screen would not transfer without close-ups—especially since it could not be interrupted, as it was in the film, by the excited counterpoint of Constanze's carriage dashing towards her dying husband through the night, or any other equivalent suspense.

Perhaps I should have attempted it, but my intuitive reluctance, together with the total alteration of the play's plotline such a plan would involve—collapse of Mozart in the opera house, et cetera—cooled me off, and I returned to renewed work on the same masked Messenger scene I had been tussling with seventeen years before.

The work I did in Stratford was really not radical enough, but it did start me thinking very seriously about how I could humanize Salieri more—removing what I was coming to think of as a betraying coarseness in the use of the masked figure, and deepening his emotions when he is confronted in the end with his palpably dying victim.

THE FIFTH (AND SIXTH) VERSION

So we come finally to what is published here for the first time: the last work on the Last Encounter, done for the admirable revival of 1998 at the Old Vic Theatre in London, with some absolutely vital additions the following year when it transferred (via Los Angeles) to Broadway.

To my great satisfaction, Peter Hall agreed to direct again; the extremely skilled David Suchet played Salieri with a totally persuasive truthfulness, nightly evoking a tremendous personal reception in both cities; and the brilliant Michael Sheen appeared as a superbly credible hyperactive Mozart. My only regret about the production was that the Lincoln Center in New York, entirely through lack of funds thanks to government cuts, proved unable to record the finished work on film, as it had so expertly done with the first Broadway production. This was a calamity, since for an institution of that eminence to possess *two filmed versions* of the same work, achieved by the same great director and separated by twenty years, would have constituted a rare gift to all serious students of theater and given a wonderful example of the proper usefulness of a cultural archive.

I believe these final rewrites of this most troublesome scene were ultimately the best of the many I undertook. They represent a huge rethinking of the whole trajectory of action concerning Salieri's growing guilt, which I had long wanted to explore in greater depth: a need for atonement, first broached in the earliest production with Scofield, more and more urgently arising in the man from his realization of what he has actually done with his own self-debasing life.

To prepare for the necessary alteration in my villain's implacable destructiveness, I had first to reconceive the episode where the two men go together to *The Magic Flute*, substituting for the great choral outburst at the end of Act Two the infinitely serene song for Prince Tamino in Act One when he literally plays on the magic flute he has been given and wild animals draw near to listen: "*Wie stark ist nicht dein Zauberton!*" Sitting on his bench Salieri also becomes enchanted—moved to a hitherto unexperienced wonder that such sweet exaltation can issue from a man whom he has deliberately reduced to ruin. Instinctively he reaches up to grasp Mozart's hand, only to be prevented by a furious interruption he himself has brought about: Baron van Swieten appears, scandalized at discovering his cherished Masonic secrets exposed in a theatrical vaudeville. From this moment, the seeds of *shame* start to grow in Salieri, leading ineluctably to a desperate need to acquire some sort of forgiveness—not from God but from Man: Mozart.

The rejection of Mozart by the Masons (an obviously fictional event, though there were persistent rumors in the ensuing two cen-

turies that some of the Brotherhood had been deeply displeased by
the vaudeville and its indiscreet composer) is the final and most
lethal injury engineered by Salieri in the play. The Venticelli now
report to him that the poor man has shut himself away in his
apartment, seeing nobody, yet glimpsed continually at his window
staring down wildly into the street, as if expecting something—*or
someone*. The gossip in Vienna is that Mozart has lost his wits.
Salieri is suddenly galvanized: loss of wits would surely mean loss
of talent! Excited and horrified as well that he might have literally
driven a man mad, he muffles himself in his cloak and hurries
across the freezing city at dead of night to spy on him in secret.

What follows is almost farcical, as unexpectedly the moon
comes out to expose him staring up from the dingy alley, and a
seemingly demented Mozart calls down an infantile little rhyme
inviting him to enter the "Palazzo Amadeo." Salieri has no choice
but to climb his stairs. And so their Last Encounter begins. There
is really no need for me to describe this hugely emotional meeting
between the two men in detail here, since it is to be found in its
rightful place in this book, published for the first time. I would like
only to point out the enormous differences in the scene from anything that was ever played in previous Versions, which made it for
me supremely worth doing.

As soon as Salieri enters the chamber which is Mozart's last
lodging, and looks upon the foul place to which his machinations
have consigned him, he sees also, strewn across the floor, a pavement of manuscripts—and of course guesses instantly what Wolfgang has been doing all this time alone. He is actually engaged in
writing the Requiem to present to that ghostly Messenger whom
he has already described, and who Salieri (along with the audience) of course believes does not exist. And now he is even more
shaken as the unstrung man confesses his conviction that he is
writing this music for his own death. The idea of death in fact
invades the room in a startling way. With deep apprehension (as in
all previous Versions but now with a very different result) Salieri is

persuaded to read the Kyrie—and experiences the most harrowing moment of his life.

The music is appalling. He holds in his hand an unnerving contradiction: something indestructible yet rotting, immortal yet stinking of death. *But whose?* . . . As the terrible chorus fills his head with its reverberating despair, he is seized with a sickening realization. It is sounding not for Mozart but for a Boy: that eager, innocent boy he himself once was, stumbling round the fields of Lombardy singing his apprentice anthems up to the God he ached to serve—now destroyed forever by his own unrelenting malice. Only then does he urgently seek Mozart's pardon.

And now comes the most bitter consequence. Desperate, Salieri tries to confess, even begging for forgiveness on his knees to an increasingly terrified victim, who in self-protection is palpably regressing before him into childish avoidance. The more urgently he declares his guilt, the more Mozart sings his father's little goodnight "Kissing Song," over and over again, to exclude all possible knowledge of what is being told him, until finally Salieri gives up in defeat and leaves—denied any form of absolution. We are a long way from the 1980 scene on Broadway with Ian McKellen yelling down, "Leave me—alone! Alone!" through the table under which Mozart sits cowering—undeniably effective as that was.

Of course it is a different kind of effectiveness with which this alteration is concerned. It seems to me the play is moved from high melodrama into a more credible area, akin to tragedy. This was certainly my intention, eagerly abetted by the director and the leading actor, both of whom were not merely supportive but passionately grateful for all the new writing coming their way. From the beginning, it had been Mr. Suchet's greatest desire to palliate the monstrosity in Salieri with a strong dose of familiarity, so that his audience could actually recognize *themselves* in the character. These rewrites allowed him to do that. Salieri remained a cunning assassin but emerged as more complex. One now received a clearer sense of what it might feel like to be a man for whom Music is Life, yet who rises every morning with the fixed determination to destroy its finest manifestation. I always wanted him to be what he called himself—"A good man, as the world calls Good"—corrupted by an unassuageable need to be a vessel for the Great: a nature turning evil through an infatuation with an Absolute. Even an archvillain like Richard III has his nightmare of self-confrontation in his tent on the night before the battle: the ghosts of those he has murdered arise and denounce him, all with the same phrase—"Despair and die!" Salieri's tent is that freezing, filthy room in the Rauhensteingasse, and the Requiem intones to him the same damning injunction.

I know that to some people my attempts to escape from unalloyed melodrama are unwelcome, and part of me sympathizes with them. I actually adore melodrama—the world of masks and muffled figures at midnight, and especially the enlarged gestures on which theater thrives, for which I believe it is still most properly loved. This is why I restored in this published version the wildest moment, when Salieri *ate* a piece of the Requiem. I missed this sorely in our revival, because it really belonged there and should never have been omitted. But I did not miss (or perhaps missed just a little) his standing cloaked in that dingy alley with upraised fingers ticking off the time left for Mozart to complete his Death Mass. That always seemed to me to be forced. The most extreme genres, like melodrama or farce, have the most palpable limitations, to be ignored at the peril of discrediting them.

And now, before concluding my observations on this final, Final Encounter, I have one last, considerable change in it to reveal. For the pages in this volume, and all subsequent copies, I have inserted not merely Salieri's chewing of the Kyrie but, a few minutes later in the action, some totally new additions which I now consider vital. As I worked on this whole scene for publication, I came to realise that, longer as it already was than any of the other performed Versions described in this Preface, it was actually *not long enough*. Essentially, the way Salieri's emotional journey was charted after he had embarked on his attempt to get absolution from Mozart appeared to me, on reviewing it, too compressed. It seemed almost over before it started.

At the risk of prolonging the encounter too much for the play to bear, I knew I had to give its unfolding a more expansive rhythm. Chiefly I felt I had to deal more fully with the ambiguity of Salieri's anguish—and also to accommodate what must surely by now be a need in the audience to hear this wretched man, standing before his victim, offer not only contrition but some fierce words of *self-justification* as well.

A few of these words (referring to the indifference of God) are actually reproduced from the 1980 Broadway version where they were spoken with memorable intensity by Ian McKellen; the majority, however, are new. As a result, I believe I have now achieved a realer exchange between the two and also—though I have not actually heard it all acted out on a stage—that the added stretch of dramatic action will give it a more powerful charge of theatrical suspense. This last quality is essential: it is, after all, the drama's true climax, wherein my corrupt chief protagonist is clearly seen to be foiled in his desperate attempt to gain forgiveness, which generates the finale of the place.

In his disturbed head, Salieri would naturally attribute his defeat to the intervention of God. Hence—after thirty-two increasingly anguished years—he would finally come to hatch his demented counterattack: a desperate attempt to achieve, through false confession followed by suicide, in place of absolution an infamous immortality. This constitutes the man's last pathetic plot, put into motion at the very beginning of the play (when he is heard crying out for all Vienna to hear: *"Mozart, pardon your assassin!"*)—which of course is also foiled, even more humiliatingly, at the very end of it.

A playwright lucky enough to have his work done in several large cities in several different Versions over several years cannot really be blamed for repeatedly considering textual material as it reappears—scrutinizing it through the glasses of Then and Now, as perspectives change and with them his own taste. Indeed, sometimes I wonder at those writers who display no desire to alter anything when work is revived. And sometimes, too, I envy their seeming certitude—or even their indifference, which may be a form of instinctive wisdom!

Critics or perceptive friends are of little help in this, mainly because they recall—or more often misrecall—a past Version with a fondness that will automatically exclude all one's efforts to alter it. In the case of *Amadeus,* on the one hand, many strangers in the audiences confessed to me they were strongly moved by this latest reshaping, and I could see in their eyes how this was true. On the other hand, there were others who prefer being appalled, in the deepest sense, to being moved. It is hard to judge between such reactions; although one should always remember when appraising tragedy that Aristotle spoke not only of terror but also of pity. Certainly it has to be recorded here that the "new" play was greeted *every night* of its nine-month run at the Old Vic Theatre with a rapturous standing ovation—a rare sight in London at a play—and with the same athletic accolade on Broadway.

Perhaps the last word on all this really belongs to Peter Hall, who is in a position to know the piece rather well, having directed all leading stage versions in England and America. He regards the play now, in his own words, not only as "immeasurably improved" but also as "finished." If I don't agree with him publicly here in print, it is only because I may well ask him to direct it again in another twenty years, and would need to have something in reserve with which to tempt him.

THE SET

Amadeus can be played in a variety of settings. What is described here is to a large extent based on the exquisite formulation found for the play by the designer John Bury, helped into being by the director, Peter Hall.

This is not to denigrate in any way the superbly original set designed twenty years later for this newly published Version by the brilliant William Dudley, which I shall always remember with pleasure. I choose to describe Bury's set again here partly as a tribute to this most dazzling career but also in *hommage* to the man himself, who died in November 2000 after a long and distressing illness. John was a fine, hugely talented man and a great designer.

The set consisted basically of a handsome rectangle of patterned wood, its longest sides leading away from the viewer, set into a stage of ice-blue plastic. This surface shifted beguilingly under various lights played upon it, to show gunmetal grey, or azure, or emerald green, and reflected the actors standing upon it. The entire design was undeniably modern, yet it suggested without self-consciousness the age of the Rococo. Costumes and objects were sumptuously of the period, and should always be so wherever the play is produced.

The rectangle largely represented interiors: especially those of Salieri's salon; Mozart's last apartment; assorted reception rooms and opera houses. At the back stood a grand proscenium sporting gilded cherubs blowing huge trumpets, and supporting grand curtains of sky blue, which could rise and part to reveal an enclosed space almost the width of the area downstage. Into this space superb backdrops were flown, and superb projections thrown, to show the scarlet boxes of theaters, or a vast wall of gold mirrors with an immense golden fireplace, representing the encrusted Royal Palace. In it also appeared silhouettes of scandalmongering citizens of Vienna, or the formal figures of the Emperor Joseph II of Austria and his brocaded courtiers. This wonderful upstage space, which was in effect an immense Rococo peep show, will be referred to throughout this text as the Light Box.

On stage, before the lights are lowered in the theater, four objects are to be seen by the audience. To the left, on the wooden rectangle, stands a small table, bearing a cake-stand. In the center, farther upstage and also on the wood, stands a wheelchair of the eighteenth century, with its back to us. To the right, on the reflecting plastic, stands a beautiful fortepiano in a marquetry case. Above the stage is suspended a large chandelier showing many globes of opaque glass.

All directions will be given from the viewpoint of the audience.

Changes of time and place are indicated throughout by changes of light.

In reading the text it must be remembered that the action is wholly continuous. Its fluidity is ensured by the use of servants played by actors in eighteenth-century livery, whose role it is to move the furniture and carry on props with ease and correctness, while the action proceeds around them. Through a pleasant paradox of theater their constant coming and going, bearing tables, chairs or cloaks, should render them virtually invisible, and certainly unremarkable. This will aid the play to be acted throughout in its proper manner; with the sprung line, gracefulness and energy for which Mozart is so especially celebrated.

AUTHOR'S NOTE

The *'s which now and then divide the page indicate changes of Scene: but there is to be no interruption. The scenes must flow into one another without pause from the beginning to the end of the play.

P.S.

CHARACTERS

ANTONIO SALIERI

WOLFGANG AMADEUS MOZART

CONSTANZE WEBER, *wife to Mozart*

JOSEPH II, *Emperor of Austria*

COUNT JOHANN KILIAN VON STRACK, Royal Chamberlain

COUNT FRANZ ORSINI-ROSENBERG, *Director of the Imperial Opera*

BARON GOTTFRIED VAN SWIETEN, *Prefect of the Imperial Library*

TWO "VENTICELLI"—*"Little Winds," purveyors of information, gossip and rumor*

A MAJORDOMO

SALIERI'S VALET (Silent part)

SALIERI'S COOK (Silent part)

KAPELLMEISTER BONNO (Silent part)

TERESA SALIERI, *wife of Salieri* (Silent part)

KATHERINA CAVALIERI, *Salieri's pupil* (Silent part)

CITIZENS OF VIENNA

The VENTICELLI also play the TWO GALLANTS at the party in Act One.

The CITIZENS OF VIENNA also play the SERVANTS, who move furniture and bring on props as required.

The action of the play takes place in Vienna in November 1823 and, in recall, the decade 1781–1791.

SCENE I

Vienna

[*Darkness.*
*Savage whispers fill the theater. We can distinguish nothing
at first from this snakelike hissing save the word* Salieri!
*repeated here, there and everywhere around the theater. Also,
the barely distinguishable word* Assassin!

*The whispers overlap and increase in volume, slashing
the air with wicked intensity. Then the light grows upstage to
reveal the silhouettes of men and women dressed in the top
hats and skirts of the early nineteenth century—*CITIZENS OF
VIENNA, *all crowded together in the Light Box, and uttering
their scandal.*]

WHISPERERS: *Salieri! . . . Salieri! . . . Salieri!*

[*Upstage, in a wheelchair, with his back to us, sits an old
man. We can just see, as the light grows a little brighter, the
top of his head, encased in an old red cap, and perhaps the
shawl wrapped around his shoulders.*]

Salieri! . . . Salieri! . . . Salieri!

[*Two middle-aged gentlemen hurry in from either side, also
wearing the long cloaks and tall hats of the period. These are
the two* VENTICELLI: *purveyors of fact, rumor and gossip
throughout the play. They speak rapidly—in this first appear-
ance extremely rapidly—so that the scene has the air of a fast*

and dreadful overture. Sometimes they speak to each other,
sometimes to us—but always with the urgency of men who
have ever been first with the news.]

VENTICELLO 1: I don't believe it.

VENTICELLO 2: I don't believe it.

V.1: I don't believe it.

V.2: I don't believe it.

WHISPERERS: *Salieri!*

V.1: They say.

V.2: I hear.

V.1: I hear.

V.2: They say.

V.1 & V.2: *I don't believe it!*

WHISPERERS: *Salieri!*

V.1: The whole city is talking.

V.2: You hear it all over.

V.1: The cafés.

V.2: The Opera.

V.1: The Prater.

V.2: The gutter.

V.1: They say even Metternich repeats it.

V.2: They say even Beethoven, his old pupil.

V.1: But why now?

V.2: After so long?

V.1: Thirty-two years!

V.1 & V.2: *I don't believe it!*

WHISPERERS: SALIERI!

V.1: They say he shouts it out all day!

V.2: I hear he cries it out all night!

V.1: Stays in his apartments.

V.2: Never goes out.

v.1: Not for a year now.

v.2: Longer. Longer.

v.1: Must be seventy.

v.2: Older. Older.

v.1: Antonio Salieri—

v.2: The famous musician—

v.1: Shouting it aloud!

v.2: Crying it aloud!

v.1: Impossible.

v.2: Incredible.

v.1: I don't believe it!

v.2: I don't believe it!

WHISPERERS: SALIERI!

v.1: I know who *started* the tale!

v.2: *I* know who started the tale!

> [*Two old men—one thin and dry, one very fat—detach themselves from the crowd at the back and walk downstage, on either side: Salieri's* VALET *and* PASTRY COOK.]

v.1: [*Indicating him*]. The old man's valet!

v.2: [*Indicating him*]. The old man's cook!

v.1: The valet hears him shouting!

v.2: The cook hears him crying!

v.1: What a story!

v.2: What a scandal!

> [*The* VENTICELLI *move quickly upstage, one on either side, and each collects a silent informant.* VENTICELLO ONE *walks down eagerly with the* VALET; VENTICELLO TWO *walks down eagerly with the* COOK.]

v.1: [*To* VALET]. What does he say, your master?

v.2: [*To* COOK]. What *exactly* does he say, the Kapellmeister?

v.1: Alone in his house—

v.2: All day and all night—

v.1: What sins does he shout?

v.2: The old fellow—

v.1: The recluse—

v.2: What horrors have you heard?

v.1 & v.2: *Tell us! Tell us! Tell us at once! What does he cry? What does he cry? What does he cry?*

    [VALET *and* COOK *gesture toward* SALIERI.]

SALIERI: [*In a great cry*]. MOZART!!!

    [*Silence*]

v.1: [*Whispering*]. Mozart!

v.2: [*Whispering*]. Mozart!

SALIERI: *Perdonami, Mozart! Il tuo assassino ti chiede perdono!*

v.1: [*In disbelief*]. Pardon, Mozart!

v.2: [*In disbelief*]. Pardon your assassin!

v.1 & v.2: *God preserve us!*

SALIERI: *Pietà, Mozart! . . . Mozart, pietà!*

v.1: Mercy, Mozart!

v.2: Mozart, have mercy!

v.1: He speaks in Italian when excited!

v.2: German when not!

v.1: *Perdonami, Mozart!*

v.2: Pardon your assassin!

    [*The* VALET *and the* COOK *walk to either side of the stage and stand still. Pause. The* VENTICELLI *cross themselves, deeply shocked.*]

v.1: There was talk once before, you know.

v.2: Thirty-two years ago.

v.1: When Mozart was dying.

v.2: He claimed he'd been poisoned!

v.1: Some said he accused a man.

v.2: Some said that man was Salieri!

v.1: But no one believed it.

v.2: They *knew* what he died of!

v.1: Syphilis, surely.

v.2: Like everybody else.

[*Pause*]

V.I: [*Slyly*]. But what if Mozart was right?

V.2: If he really *was* murdered?

V.I: And by him. Our First Kapellmeister!

V.2: Antonio Salieri!

V.I: It can't possibly be true.

V.2: It's not actually credible.

V.I: Because *why?*

V.2: Because why?

V.I & V.2: *Why on earth would he do it?*

V.I: And why confess *now?*

V.2: After thirty-two years!

WHISPERERS: *Salieri!*

[*Pause*]

SALIERI: *Mozart! Mozart! Perdonami!* . . . *Il tuo assassino ti chiede perdono!*

[*Pause. They look at him, then at each other.*]

V.I: What do you think?

V.2: What do you think?

V.I: I don't believe it!

V.2: *I* don't believe it!

[*Pause*]

V.I: All the same . . .

V.2: Is it just possible?

V.I & V.2: [*Whispering*]. *Did he do it after all?!*

WHISPERERS: SALIERI!

[*The* VENTICELLI *go off. The* VALET *and the* COOK *remain, on either side of the stage.* SALIERI *swivels his wheelchair around and stares at us. We see a man of seventy in an old stained dressing gown with an old Turkish-style turban on his head. He rises and squints at the audience, as if trying to see it.*]

SCENE 2

Salieri's Apartment.
November 1823. The small hours.

SALIERI: [*Calling to audience*]. *Vi saluto! Ombri del Futuro! Anto-nio Salieri—a vostro servizio!*

[*A clock outside in the street strikes three.*]

I can almost see you in your ranks—waiting for your turn to live. Ghosts of the Future! Be visible. I beg you. Be visible. Come to this dusty old room—this time, the smallest hours of dark November, eighteen hundred and twenty-three—and be my confessors! Will you not enter this place and stay with me till dawn? Just till dawn—smeary six o'clock!

WHISPERERS: *Salieri! . . . Salieri! . . .*

[*The curtains slowly descend on the* CITIZENS OF VIENNA. *Faint images of long windows are projected on the silk.*]

SALIERI: Can you hear them? Vienna is a City of Slander. Everyone tells tales here: even my servants. I keep only two now. [*He indicates them.*] They've been with me ever since I came here, fifty years ago. The keeper of the razor; the maker of the cakes. One keeps me tidy, the other keeps me full. [*To them*] "Leave me, both of you! Tonight I do not go to bed at all!"

[*They react in surprise.*]

"Return here tomorrow morning at six precisely—to shave, to feed your capricious master!" [*He smiles at them both and claps his hands in dismissal.*] *Via. Via, via, via! Grazie!*

[*They bow, bewildered, and leave the stage. He peers hard at the audience, trying to see it.*]

Now, won't you appear! I need you—*desperately!* This is the last hour of my life. Those about to die implore you! . . . What must I do to make you visible? Raise you up in the flesh to be my last, last audience? . . . Does it take an Invocation? That's

how it's always done in opera! Ah yes, of course: that's it. An
Invocation. The only way. [*He rises.*] Let me try to conjure you
now—Ghosts of the distant Future—so I can see you.

[*He gets out of the wheelchair and huddles over to the
fortepiano. He stands at the instrument and begins to sing in
a high cracked voice, interrupting himself at the end of each
sentence with figurations on the keyboard in the manner of a
recitativo secco. During this, the house lights slowly come up
to illuminate the audience.*]

[*Singing*]

Ghosts of the future!

Shades of time to come!

So much more unavoidable than those of time gone by!

Appear with what sympathy incarnation may endow you!

Appear you:

The yet to be born!

The yet to hate!

The yet to *kill!*

Appear . . . posterity!

[*The light on the audience reaches its maximum. It stays like
this during all of the following.*]

[*Speaking again*] There. It worked. I can see you! That is the
result of proper training. I was taught invocation by Gluck, who
was a true master at it. He had to be. In his day, that was what
people went to the opera for: the raising of gods, and ghosts.
Nowadays, since Rossini became the rage, they prefer to watch ♩
the escapades of hairdressers. [*Pause*] *Scusate.* Invocation is an
exhausting business! I need refreshment. [*He sits again in his
wheelchair, moves himself over to the cake-stand, selects a cake
and eats it.*] It's a little repellent, I admit, but actually, the first
sin I have to confess to you is gluttony. Sticky gluttony at that.
Infantine, *Italian* gluttony! The truth is that all my life I have
never been able to conquer a lust for the sweetmeats of North-
ern Italy, where I was born. From the ages of three to seventy-

three, my entire career has been conducted to the taste of almonds sprinkled with sifted sugar. [*Lustfully*] Veronese biscuits! Milanese macaroons! Snow dumplings with pistachio sauce! . . . Do not judge me too harshly for this. All men harbor patriotic feelings of some kind. . . . My parents were provincial subjects of the Austrian Empire. A Lombardy merchant and his Lombardy wife. Their notion of place was the tiny town of Legnago—which I could not wait to leave. Their notion of God was a superior Habsburg emperor, inhabiting a Heaven only slightly farther off than Vienna. All they required of Him was to protect commerce, and keep them forever preserved in *mediocrity*. . . . My own requirements were very different. [*Pause*] I wanted *Fame*. Not to deceive you, I wanted to blaze like a comet across the firmament of Europe! Yet only in one especial way. Music! Absolute music! . . . A note of music is either right or wrong *absolutely!* Not even time can alter that: music is God's art. [*Excited by the recollection*] Already when I was ten a spray of sounded notes would make me dizzy almost to falling! By twelve, I was stumbling about the fields of Lombardy humming my arias and anthems to the Lord. My one desire was to join all the composers who had celebrated His glory through the long Italian past! . . . Every Sunday I saw Him in church, painted on the flaking wall. I don't mean Christ. The Christs of Lombardy are simpering sillies, with lambkins in their arms. No: I mean an old candle-smoked God in a mulberry robe, staring at the world with dealer's eyes. Tradesmen had put him up there. Those eyes made bargains, real and irreversible. "You give me so—I'll give you so! No more. No less!" [*He eats a sweet biscuit in his excitement.*] The night before I left Legnago forever, I went to see Him, and made a bargain with Him myself! I was a sober sixteen, filled with a desperate sense of *right*. I knelt before the God of Bargains, and I prayed through the moldering plaster with all my soul.

[*He kneels.*]

"*Signore*, let me be a composer! Grant me sufficient fame to enjoy it. In return, I will live with virtue. I will strive to better the lot of my fellows. And I will honor You with much music all the days of my life!" As I said *Amen*, I saw His eyes flare. [As "*God*"] "*Bene*. Go forth, Antonio. Serve Me and mankind, and you will be blessed!" . . . "*Grazie!*" I called back. "I am Your servant for life!"

[*He gets to his feet again.*]

The very next day, a family friend suddenly appeared—out of the blue—took me off to Vienna and paid for me to study music!

Shortly afterwards I met the Emperor, who favored me.

Clearly my bargain had been accepted!

[*Pause*]

The same year I left Lombardy, a young prodigy was touring Europe. A miraculous virtuoso aged ten years. Wolfgang Amadeus Mozart.

[*Pause. He smiles at the audience.*]

And now, gracious ladies! obliging gentlemen! I present to you—for one performance only—my last composition, entitled *The Death of Mozart; or, Did I Do It?* . . . Dedicated to posterity on this, the last night of my life!

[*He bows deeply, undoing as he does so the buttons of his old dressing gown. When he straightens himself, divesting himself of this drab outer garment and his cap, he is a man in the prime of life, wearing a sky-blue coat and the elegant decent clothes of a successful composer of the 1780s. The house lights go down again on the audience.*]

SCENE 3

Transformation to the Eighteenth Century

[*Music sounds softly in the background: a serene piece for
strings by Salieri.* SERVANTS *enter. One takes away the dressing gown and cap; another places on the table a wig-stand
bearing a powdered wig; a third brings on a chair and places
it at the left, upstage.*

At the back, the blue curtains rise and part to show the
EMPEROR JOSEPH II *and his* COURT *bathed in golden light,
against a golden background of mirrors and an immense
golden fireplace. His Majesty is seated, holding a rolled
paper, listening to the music. Also listening are* COUNT VON
STRACK; COUNT ORSINI-ROSENBERG; BARON VAN SWIETEN;
and an anonymous PRIEST, *dressed in a soutane. An old
wigged* COURTIER *enters and takes his place at the keyboard:*
KAPELLMEISTER BONNO.]

SALIERI: [*In a young man's voice: vigorous and confident*]. The
place throughout is Vienna. The year—to begin with—1781.
The age still that of the Enlightenment: that clear time before
the guillotine fell in France and cut all our lives in half. I am
thirty-one. Already a prolific composer to the Habsburg court. I
own a respectable house and a respectable wife—Teresa.

[*Enter* TERESA: *a padded, placid lady who seats herself
uprightly in the upstage chair.*]

I do not mock her, I assure you. I required only one quality in a
domestic companion—lack of fire. And in that omission Teresa
was conspicuous. [*Ceremoniously, he puts on his powdered
wig.*] I also had a prize pupil: Katherina Cavalieri.

[KATHERINA *swirls on from the opposite side: a beautiful girl
of twenty. The music becomes vocal: faintly, we hear a*
SOPRANO *singing a concert aria. Like* TERESA's, KATHERINA's

*part is mute, but as she enters she stands by the fortepiano
and energetically mimes her rapturous singing. At the keyboard, old* BONNO *accompanies her appreciatively.*]

She was later to become the best singer of her age. But at that
time she was mainly a bubbling student with merry eyes and a
sweet, eatable mouth. I was very much in love with Katherina—
or at least in lust. But because of my vow to God I was entirely
faithful to my wife. I had never laid a finger upon the girl—
except occasionally to depress her diaphragm in the way of
teaching her to sing. My ambition burned with an unquench-
able flame. Its chief goal was the post of First Royal Kapellmeister, then held by Giuseppe Bonno [*Indicating him*], seventy
years old, and apparently immortal.

[*All on stage, save* SALIERI, *suddenly freeze. He speaks very
directly to the audience.*]

You, when you come, will be told that we musicians of the eighteenth century were no better than servants: the willing slaves of
the well-to-do. This is quite true. It is also quite false. Yes, we
were servants. But we were learned servants! And we used our
learning to celebrate men's average lives.

[*A grander music sounds. The* EMPEROR *remains seated, but
the other four men in the Light Box*—STRACK, ROSENBERG,
VAN SWIETEN *and the* PRIEST—*come slowly out onto the
main stage and process imposingly down it, and around it,
and up it again to return to their places. Only the* PRIEST *goes
off, as do* TERESA *on her side, and* KATHERINA *on hers.*]

[*Over this*] We took unremarkable men—usual bankers, run-of-
the-mill officials, ordinary soldiers and statesmen and wives—
and sacramentalized their mediocrity. We smoothed their noons
with strings *divisi!* We pierced their nights with *chitarrini!* We
gave them processions for their strutting, serenades for their
rutting, high horns for their hunting and drums for their wars!
Trumpets sounded when they entered the world, and trombones
groaned when they left it! The savor of their days remains

behind because of *us,* our music still remembered while their politics are long forgotten.

[*The* EMPEROR *hands his rolled paper to* STRACK *and goes off. In the Light Box are left standing, like three icons,* ROSEN-BERG, *plump and supercilious, aged sixty;* STRACK, *stiff and proper, aged fifty-five;* VAN SWIETEN, *cultivated and serious, aged fifty. The lights go down on them a little.*]

Tell me, before you call us servants, who served whom? And who, I wonder, in your generations, will immortalize *you?*

[*The two* VENTICELLI *come on quickly downstage, from either side. They now appear younger also, and are dressed well, in the style of the late eighteenth century. Their manner is more confidential than before.*]

V.1: [*To* SALIERI]. Sir!

V.2: [*To* SALIERI]. Sir!

V.1: [*To* SALIERI]. Sir. Sir.

V.2: [*To* SALIERI]. Sir. Sir. Sir!

[SALIERI *bids them wait for a second.*]

SALIERI: I was the most successful young musician in the city of musicians. And now suddenly, without warning—

[*They approach him eagerly, from either side.*]

V.1: Mozart!

V.2: Mozart!

V.1 & V.2: *Mozart has come!*

SALIERI: These are my *Venticelli.* My "Little Winds," as I called them. [*He gives each a coin from his pocket.*] The secret of successful living in a large city is always to know to the minute what is being done behind your back.

V.1: He's left Salzburg.

V.2: Means to give concerts.

V.1: Asking for subscribers.

SALIERI: I'd known of him for years, of course. Tales of his prowess were told all over Europe.

V.1: They say he wrote his first symphony at five.

v.2: I hear his first concerto at four.

v.1: A full opera at fourteen!

SALIERI: [*To them*]. How old is he now?

v.2: Twenty-five.

SALIERI: [*Carefully*]. And how long is he remaining?

v.1: He's not departing.

v.2: He's here to stay.

    [*The* VENTICELLI *glide off.*]

SCENE 4

The Palace of Schönbrunn

[*Lights come up on the three stiff figures of* ROSENBERG, STRACK *and* VAN SWIETEN, *standing upstage in the Light Box. The* CHAMBERLAIN *hands the paper he has received from the* EMPEROR *to the* DIRECTOR OF THE OPERA. SALIERI *remains downstage.*]

STRACK: [*To* ROSENBERG]. You are required to commission a comic opera in German from Herr Mozart.

SALIERI: [*To audience*]. Johann von Strack. Royal Chamberlain. A court official to his collarbone.

ROSENBERG: [*Loftily*]. Why in German? Italian is the only possible language for opera!

SALIERI: Count Orsini-Rosenberg. Director of the Opera. Benevolent to all things Italian—especially myself.

STRACK: [*Firmly*]. The idea of a national opera is dear to His Majesty's heart. He desires to hear pieces in good plain German.

VAN SWIETEN: Yes, but why *comic*? It is not the function of music to be funny.

SALIERI: Baron van Swieten. Prefect of the Imperial Library.

Ardent Freemason. Yet to find *anything* funny. Known, for his enthusiasm for old-fashioned music, as "Lord Fugue."

VAN SWIETEN: I heard last week a remarkable *serious* opera from Mozart: *Idomeneo, King of Crete.*

ROSENBERG: I heard that too. A young fellow trying to impress beyond his abilities. Too much spice. Too many notes.

STRACK: [*Firmly, to* ROSENBERG]. Nevertheless, kindly convey the commission to him today.

ROSENBERG: [*Taking the paper reluctantly*]. I believe we are going to have trouble with this young man.

[ROSENBERG *leaves the Light Box and strolls down the stage to* SALIERI.]

He was a child prodigy. That always spells trouble. His father is Leopold Mozart, a bad-tempered Salzburg musician who dragged the boy endlessly round Europe, making him play the keyboard blindfolded, with one finger, and that sort of thing. [*To* SALIERI] All prodigies are hateful—*non è vero, Compositore?*

SALIERI: *Divengono sempre sterili con gli anni.*

ROSENBERG: *Precisamente. Precisamente.*

STRACK: [*Calling suspiciously*]. What are you saying?

ROSENBERG: [*Airily*]. Nothing, Herr Chamberlain! . . . *Niente, Signor Pomposo!* . . .

[*He strolls on out.* STRACK *strides off, irritated.* VAN SWIETEN *now comes downstage.*]

VAN SWIETEN: We meet tomorrow, I believe, on your committee to devise pensions for old musicians.

SALIERI: [*Deferentially*]. It's most gracious of you to attend, Baron.

VAN SWIETEN: You're a worthy man, Salieri. You should join our Brotherhood of Masons. We would welcome you warmly.

SALIERI: I would be honored, Baron!

VAN SWIETEN: If you wished, I could arrange initiation into my lodge.

SALIERI: That would be more than my due.

VAN SWIETEN: Nonsense. We embrace men of talent of all condi-
tions. I may invite young Mozart also—dependent on the
impression he makes.

SALIERI: [*Bowing*]. Of course, Baron.

[VAN SWIETEN *goes out.*]

[*To audience*] Honor indeed! In those days almost every man of
influence in Vienna was a Mason, and the Baron's lodge by far
the most fashionable. As for young Mozart, I confess I was
alarmed by his coming. Not by the commission of a comic
opera, even though I myself was then attempting one called *The
Stolen Bucket.* . . . No, what worried me were reports about the
man himself. He was praised altogether too much.

[*The* VENTICELLI *hurry in from either side.*]

V.1: Such gaiety of spirit!

V.2: Such ease of manner!

V.1: Such natural charm!

SALIERI: [*To the* VENTICELLI]. Really? Where does he live?

V.1: Peter Platz.

V.2: Number eleven.

V.1: The landlady is Madame Weber.

V.2: A real bitch.

V.1: Takes in male lodgers, and has a tribe of daughters.

V.2: Mozart is after one of them.

V.1: Constanze.

V.2: Flighty little piece.

V.1: Her mother's pushing marriage.

V.2: His *father* isn't!

V.1: Daddy is worried sick!

V.2: Writes him every day from Salzburg!

SALIERI: [*To them*]. I want to meet him. What houses does he visit?

V.1: He'll be at the Baroness Waldstädten's tomorrow night.

SALIERI: *Grazie.*

V.2: Some of his music is to be played.

SALIERI: [*To both*]. *Restiamo in contatto.*

v.1 & v.2: *Certamente, Signore!*
      [*They go off.*]
SALIERI: [*To audience*]. So to the Baroness Waldstädten's I went.
That night changed my life.

SCENE 5

The Library of the Baroness Waldstädten

[*In the Light Box, two elegantly curtained windows sur-
rounded by handsome subdued wallpaper.*
Two SERVANTS *bring on a large table loaded with cakes and
desserts. Two more carry on a grand high-backed wing chair,
which they place ceremoniously downstage at the left.*]
SALIERI: [*To audience*]. I entered the library to take first a little
refreshment. My generous hostess always put out the most
delicious confections in that room whenever she knew I was
coming. *Dolci, caramelli*, and most especially a miraculous
crema al mascarpone—which is simply cream cheese mixed
with granulated sugar and suffused with rum—that was totally
irresistible!
      [*He takes a little bowl of it from the cake-stand and sits in
      the wing chair, facing out front. Thus seated, he is invisible to
      anyone entering from upstage.*]
I had just sat down in a high-backed chair to consume this par-
adisal dish—unobservable, as it happened, to anyone who
might come in.
      [*Offstage, noises are heard.*]
CONSTANZE: [*Off*]. Squeak! Squeak! Squeak!
      [CONSTANZE *runs on from upstage: a pretty girl in her early
      twenties, full of high spirits. At this second she is pretending*

*to be a mouse. She runs across the stage in her gay party
dress, squeaking, and hides under the fortepiano.*

*Suddenly a small, pallid, large-eyed man in a showy set of
clothes runs in after her and freezes—center—as a cat would
freeze, hunting a mouse. This is* WOLFGANG AMADEUS MOZART.
*As we get to know him through his next scenes, we discover
several things about him: he is an extremely restless man, his
voice, light and high; his manner, excitable and volatile.*]

MOZART: Miaouw!

CONSTANZE: [*Betraying where she is*]. Squeak!

MOZART: Miaouw! . . . Miaouw! . . . Miaouw!

[*The composer drops on all fours and, wrinkling his face,
begins spitting and stalking his prey. The mouse—giggling
with excitement—breaks her cover and dashes across the
floor. The cat pursues. Almost at the chair where* SALIERI *sits
concealed, the mouse turns at bay. The cat stalks her—nearer
and nearer—in its knee breeches and elaborate coat.*]

I'm going to pounce-bounce! I'm going to scrunch-munch! I'm
going to chew-poo my little mouse-wouse! I'm going to tear her
to bits with my paws-claws!

CONSTANZE: No!

MOZART: Paws-claws—paws-claws—paws-claws! *Ohh!*

[*He falls on her: she screams.*]

SALIERI: [*Dryly, to audience*]. Before I could rise, it had become
difficult to do so.

MOZART: I'm going to bite you in half with my fangs-wangs! My
little Stanzerl-wanzerl-banzerl!

[*She laughs delightedly, lying prone beneath him.*]

You're trembling! . . . I think you're frightened of puss-
wuss! . . . I think you're scared to death! [*Intimately*] I think
you're going to shit yourself!

[*She squeals but is not really shocked. He emits a little baby-
ish giggle.*]

In a moment it's going to be on the floor!

CONSTANZE: Sssh! Someone'll hear you!

[*He imitates the noise of a fart.*]

Stop it, Wolferl! Ssh! . . .

MOZART: Here it comes now! I can here it *coming!* . . . Oh, what a melancholy note! Something's dropping from your boat!

[*Another fart noise, slower.* CONSTANZE *shrieks with amusement.*]

CONSTANZE: Stop it now! It's stupid! Really *stupid!*

[SALIERI *sits appalled.*]

MOZART: Hey—hey—what's "Trazom"?

CONSTANZE: What?

MOZART: T-r-a-z-o-m. What's that mean?

CONSTANZE: How should *I* know?

MOZART: It's Mozart spelled backwards—shit-wit! If you ever married me, you'd be Constanze Trazom.

CONSTANZE: No, I wouldn't.

MOZART: Yes, you would. Because I'd want everything backwards once I was married. I'd want to lick my wife's arse instead of her face.

CONSTANZE: You're not going to lick anything at this rate. Your father's never going to give his consent to us.

[*The sense of fun deserts him instantly.*]

MOZART: And who cares about his consent?

CONSTANZE: *You* do. You care very much. You wouldn't do it without it.

MOZART: Wouldn't I?

CONSTANZE: No, you wouldn't. Because you're too scared of him. I know what he says about me. [*Solemn voice*] "If you marry that dreadful girl, you'll end up lying on straw with beggars for children!"

MOZART: [*Impulsively*]. Marry me!

CONSTANZE: Don't be silly.

MOZART: Marry me!

CONSTANZE: Are you serious?

MOZART: [*Defiantly*]. Yes! . . . Answer me this minute: yes or no! Say yes, then I can go home, shit in the bed, and shout, "I *did* it!" [*He rolls on top of her delightedly. The* MAJORDOMO *of the house stalks in, upstage.*]

MAJORDOMO: [*Imperviously*]. Her Ladyship is ready to commence.

MOZART: Ah! . . . Yes! . . . Good! [*He picks himself up, embarrassed, and helps* CONSTANZE *to rise. With an attempt at dignity*] Come, my dear. The music waits!

CONSTANZE: [*Suppressing giggles*]. Oh, by all means—Herr Trazom!

[*He takes her arm. They prance off together, followed by the disapproving* MAJORDOMO. SALIERI *sits shaken.*]

SALIERI: [*To audience*]. And then, right away, the concert began. I heard it through the door—some serenade—at first only vaguely, too horrified to attend. But presently the sound insisted—a solemn Adagio in E flat.

[*The Adagio from the Serenade for thirteen wind instruments (K. 361) begins to sound. Quietly and quite slowly, seated in the wing chair,* SALIERI *speaks over the music.*]

SALIERI: It started simply enough: just a pulse in the lowest registers—bassoons and basset horns—like a rusty squeezebox. It would have been comic except for the slowness, which gave it instead a sort of serenity. And then suddenly, high above it, sounded a single note on the oboe.

[*We hear it.*]

It hung there unwavering, piercing me through, till breath could hold it no longer, and a clarinet withdrew it out of me, and sweetened it into a phrase of such delight it had me trembling. The light flickered in the room. My eyes clouded! [*With ever-increasing emotion and vigor*] The squeezebox groaned louder, and over it the higher instruments wailed and warbled, throwing lines of sound around me— long lines of pain around and through me. Ah, the pain! Pain as I had never known it. I called

up to my sharp old God, *"What is this? . . . What?!"* But the
squeezebox went on and on, and the pain cut deeper into my
shaking head, until suddenly I was running—

[*He bolts out of the chair and runs across the stage in a fever,
to a corner, down right. Behind him in the Light Box, the
library fades into a street scene at night: small houses under a
rent sky. The music continues, fainter, underneath.*]

—dashing through the side door, stumbling downstairs into the
street, into the cold night, gasping for life. [*Calling up in agony*]
"What?! What is this? Tell me, Signore! What is this *pain?*
What is this *need* in the sound? Forever unfulfillable, yet fulfill-
ing him who hears it, utterly. Is it *Your* need? Can it be
Yours? . . ."

[*Pause*]

Dimly the music sounded from the salon above. Dimly the stars
shone on the empty street. I was suddenly frightened. It seemed
to me that I had heard a voice of God—and that it issued from
a creature whose own voice I had also heard—and it was the
voice of an obscene child!

[*Light change. The street scene fades.*]

SCENE 6

Salieri's Apartment

[*It remains dark.*]

SALIERI: I ran home and buried my fear in work. More pupils—till
there were thirty and forty. More committees to help musicians.
More motets and anthems to God's glory. And at night I prayed
for just one thing. [*He kneels desperately.*] "Let your voice enter
me! Let *me* be your conduit! . . . *Let* me!" [*Pause. He rises.*] As

for Mozart, I avoided meeting him—and sent out my Little
Winds for whatever scores of his could be found.

[*The* VENTICELLI *come in with manuscripts.* SALIERI *sits at
the fortepiano, and they show him the music alternately, as*
SERVANTS *unobtrusively remove the Waldstädten table and
wing chair.*]

V.1: Six fortepiano sonatas composed in Munich.

V.2: Two in Mannheim.

V.1: A Parisian symphony.

SALIERI: [*To audience*]. Clever. They were all clever. But yet they
seemed to me completely empty!

V.1: A Divertimento in D.

V.2: A Cassazione in G.

V.1: A Grand Litany in E flat.

SALIERI: [*To audience*]. The same. Conventional. Even boring. The
productions of a precocious youngster—Leopold Mozart's
swanky son—nothing more. That Serenade was obviously an
exception in his work: the sort of accident which might visit any
composer on a lucky day!

[*The* VENTICELLI *go off with the music.*]

Had I in fact been simply taken by surprise that the filthy creature could write music at all? . . . Suddenly I felt immensely
cheered! I would seek him out and welcome him myself to
Vienna!

SCENE 7

The Palace of Schönbrunn

[*Quick light change. The* EMPEROR *is revealed standing in
bright light before the gilded mirrors and the fireplace,*

attended by CHAMBERLAIN STRACK. *His Majesty is a dapper,
cheerful figure, aged forty, largely pleased with himself and
the world. Downstage, from opposite sides,* VAN SWIETEN
and ROSENBERG *hurry on.*]

JOSEPH: Fêtes and fireworks, gentlemen! Mozart is here! He's waiting below!

[*All bow.*]

ALL: Majesty!

JOSEPH: *Je suis follement impatient!*

SALIERI: [*To audience*]. The Emperor Joseph the Second of Austria.
Son of Maria Theresa. Brother of Marie Antoinette. Adorer of
music—provided that it made no demands upon the royal ear.
[*To the* EMPEROR, *deferentially*] Majesty, I have written a little
march in Mozart's honor. May I play it as he comes in?

JOSEPH: By all means, Court Composer. What a delightful idea!
Have you met him yet?

SALIERI: Not yet, Majesty.

JOSEPH: Fêtes and fireworks, what fun! Strack, bring him up at
once.

[STRACK *goes off. The* EMPEROR *comes onto the stage
proper.*]

Mon Dieu, I wish we could have a competition! Mozart against
some other virtuoso. Two keyboards in contest. Wouldn't that
be fun, Baron?

VAN SWIETEN: [*Stiffly*]. Not to me, Majesty. In my view, musicians
are not horses to be run against one another.

[*Slight pause*]

JOSEPH: Ah. Well—there it is.

[STRACK *returns.*]

STRACK: Herr Mozart, Majesty.

JOSEPH: Ah! Splendid! . . . [*Conspiratorially he signs to* SALIERI,
who moves quickly to the fortepiano.] Court Composer—
allons! [To STRACK] Admit him, please.

[*Instantly* SALIERI *sits at the instrument and strikes up his march on the keyboard. At the same moment* MOZART *struts in, wearing an ornate surcoat, with dress sword. The* EMPEROR *stands downstage, and as* MOZART *approaches and begins his bow, he signs to him to halt and listen. Bewildered,* MOZART *does so, becoming aware of* SALIERI *playing his March of Welcome. It is an extremely banal piece, vaguely— but only vaguely—reminiscent of another march to become very famous later on. All stand frozen in attitudes of listening, until* SALIERI *comes to a finish. Applause.*]

JOSEPH: [*To* SALIERI]. Charming . . . *Comme d'habitude!* [*He turns and extends his hand to be kissed.*] Mozart.

[MOZART *approaches, bows extravagantly, and kneels.*]

MOZART: Majesty! Your Majesty's humble slave! Let me kiss your royal hand a hundred thousand times!

[*He kisses it greedily, over and over, until its owner withdraws it in embarrassment.*]

JOSEPH: *Non, non, s'il vous plaît!* A little less enthusiasm, I beg you. Come sir, *levez-vous!* [*He assists* MOZART *to rise.*] You will not recall it, but the last time we met, you were also on the floor! My sister remembers it to this day. This young man—all of six years old, mind you—slipped on the floor at Schönbrunn—came a nasty purler on his little head. . . . Have I told you this before?

ROSENBERG: [*Hastily*]. No, Majesty!

STRACK: [*Hastily*]. No, Majesty!

SALIERI: [*Hastily*]. No, Majesty!

JOSEPH: Well, my sister Antoinette runs forward and picks him up herself. And do you know what he does? Jumps right into her arms—hoopla, just like that!—kisses her on both cheeks and says, "Will you marry me: yes or no?"

[*The* COURTIERS *laugh politely.* MOZART *giggles uncomfortably.*]

I do not mean to embarrass you, Herr Mozart. You know everyone here, surely?

MOZART: Yes, Sire. [*Bowing elaborately. To* ROSENBERG] Herr Director! [*To* VAN SWIETEN] Herr Prefect.

VAN SWIETEN: [*Warmly*]. Delighted to see you again!

JOSEPH: But not, I think, our esteemed Court Composer! . . . A most serious omission! No one who cares for art can afford not to know Herr Salieri. He wrote that exquisite little March of Welcome for you.

SALIERI: It was a trifle, Majesty.

JOSEPH: Nevertheless . . .

MOZART: [*To* SALIERI]. I'm overwhelmed, *Signore!*

JOSEPH: Ideas simply pour out of him—don't they, Strack?

STRACK: Endlessly, Sire. [*As if tipping him*] Well done, Salieri.

JOSEPH: Let it be my pleasure then to introduce you. Court Composer Salieri—Herr Mozart of Salzburg.

SALIERI: [*Sleekly, to* MOZART]. *Finalmente. Che gioia. Che diletto straordinario.*

> [*He gives him a prim bow and presents the copy of his music to the other composer, who accepts it with a flood of Italian.*]

MOZART: *Grazie, Signore! Mille milione di benvenuti! Sono commosso! E un onore eccezionale incontrare! Compositore brillante e famosissimo!* [*He makes an elaborate and showy bow in return.*]

SALIERI: [*Dryly*]. *Grazie.*

JOSEPH: Tell me, Mozart, have you received our commission for the opera?

MOZART: Indeed I have, Majesty! I am so grateful I can hardly speak! . . . I swear to you that you will have the best, the most perfect entertainment ever offered a monarch. I've already found a libretto.

ROSENBERG: [*Startled*]. Have you? I didn't hear of this!

MOZART: Forgive me, Herr Director, I entirely omitted to tell you.

ROSENBERG: May I ask why?

MOZART: It didn't seem very important.

ROSENBERG: Not important?

MOZART: Not really, no.

ROSENBERG: [*Irritated*]. It is important to *me*, Herr Mozart.

MOZART: [*Embarrassed*]. Yes, I see that. Of course.

ROSENBERG: And who, pray, is it by?

MOZART: Stephanie.

ROSENBERG: A most unpleasant man.

MOZART: But a brilliant writer.

ROSENBERG: Do you think?

MOZART: The story is really amusing, Majesty. The whole plot is set in a—[*He sniggers.*] in a . . .

JOSEPH: [*Eagerly*]. Where? Where is it set?

MOZART: It's—it's rather saucy, Majesty!

JOSEPH: Yes, yes! Where?

MOZART: Well, it's actually set in a *seraglio.*

JOSEPH: A what?

MOZART: A pasha's harem.

ROSENBERG: And you imagine that is a suitable subject for performance at a national theater?

MOZART: Yes! . . . Why not? It's very funny, it's amusing! . . . On my honor, Majesty, there's nothing offensive in it. Nothing offensive in the world. It's full of proper German virtues, I swear it!

SALIERI: [*Blandly*]. *Scusate, Signore*, but what are those? Being a foreigner, I'm not sure.

JOSEPH: You are being *cattivo*, Court Composer.

SALIERI: Not at all, Majesty.

JOSEPH: Come then, Mozart. Name us a proper German virtue!

MOZART: Love, Sire. I have yet to see that expressed in any opera.

VAN SWIETEN: Well answered, Mozart.

SALIERI: [*Smiling*]. *Scusate.* I was under the impression one rarely saw anything *else* expressed in opera.

MOZART: I mean manly love, *Signore*. Not male sopranos screeching. Or stupid couples rolling their eyes. All that absurd Italian nonsense.

[*Pause. Tension.* ROSENBERG *coughs.*]

I mean the real thing.

JOSEPH: And do you know the real thing yourself, Herr Mozart?

MOZART: Under your pardon, I think I do, Majesty.

JOSEPH: Bravo. When do you think it will be done?

MOZART: The First Act is already finished.

JOSEPH: But it can't be more than two weeks since you started!

MOZART: Composing is not hard when you have the right audience to please, Sire.

VAN SWIETEN: A charming reply, Majesty.

JOSEPH: Indeed, Baron. Fêtes and fireworks! I see we are going to have fêtes and fireworks! *Au revoir, Monsieur Mozart. Soyez bienvenu à la court.*

MOZART: [*Speaking expertly*]. *Majesté! Je suis comblé d'honneur d'être accepté dans la maison du Père de tous les musiciens! Servir un monarque aussi plein de discernement que votre Majesté, c'est un honneur qui dépasse le sommet de mes dûs!*

[*A pause. The* EMPEROR *is slightly taken aback by this flood of French.*]

JOSEPH: Ah. Well—there it is! I'll leave you gentlemen to get better acquainted.

SALIERI: Good day, Majesty.

MOZART: *Votre Majesté.*

[*They both bow.* JOSEPH *goes out.*]

ROSENBERG: Good day to you.

STRACK: Good day.

[*They follow the King.*]

VAN SWIETEN: [*Warmly shaking his hand*]. Welcome, Mozart. I shall see much more of you. Depend on it!

MOZART: Thank you.

[*He bows. The* BARON *goes.* MOZART *and* SALIERI *are left alone.*]

SALIERI: *Bene.*

MOZART: *Bene.*

SALIERI: I, too, wish you success with your opera.

MOZART: I'll have it. It's going to be superb. I must tell you I have already found the most excellent singer for the leading part.

SALIERI: Oh? Who is that?

MOZART: Her name is Cavalieri. Katherina Cavalieri. She's really German, but she thinks it will advance her career if she sports an Italian name.

SALIERI: She's quite right. It was my idea. She is in fact my prize pupil. Actually she's a very innocent child. Silly in the way of young singers—but, you know, she's only twenty.

MOZART: Yes.

> [*Without emphasis,* MOZART *freezes his movements and* SALIERI *takes one easy step forward to make a fluent aside.*]

[*To audience*] I had kept my hands off Katherina. Yes! But I could not bear to think of anyone else's upon her—least of all his!

MOZART: [*Unfreezing*]. You're a good fellow, Salieri! And that's a jolly little thing you wrote for me.

SALIERI: It was my pleasure.

MOZART: Let's see if I can remember it. May I?

SALIERI: By all means. It's yours.

MOZART: *Grazie, Signore.*

> [MOZART *tosses the manuscript onto the lid of the fortepiano, where he cannot see it, sits at the instrument and plays* SALIERI's *March of Welcome perfectly from memory—at first slowly, recalling it, but on the reprise of the tune, very much faster.*]

The rest is just the same, isn't it? [*He finishes it with insolent speed.*]

SALIERI: You have a remarkable memory.

MOZART: [*Delighted with himself*]. Grazie ancora, Signore! [*He plays the opening seven bars again, but this time stops on the interval of the fourth, and sounds it again with displeasure.*] It doesn't really *work*, that fourth, does it? . . . Let's try the third above . . . [*He does so—and smiles happily.*] Ah yes! . . . Good!

[*He repeats the new interval, leading up to it smartly with the well-known military-trumpet arpeggio which characterizes the celebrated March from* The Marriage of Figaro, *"Non più andrai." Then, using the interval—tentatively, delicately, one note at a time, in the treble—he steals into the famous tune itself.*

On and on he plays, improvising happily what is virtually the March we know now, laughing gleefully each time he comes to the amended interval of a third. SALIERI *watches him with an answering smile painted on his face.*

MOZART's *playing grows more and more exhibitionistic, revealing to the audience the formidable virtuoso he is. The whole time he himself remains totally oblivious of the offense he is giving. Finally, he finishes the March with a series of triumphant flourishes and chords.*

An ominous pause.]

SALIERI: *Scusate.* I must go.

MOZART: Really? [*Springing up and indicating the keyboard*] Why don't *you* try a variation?

SALIERI: Thank you, but I must attend on the Emperor.

MOZART: Ah.

SALIERI: It has been delightful to meet you.

MOZART: For me too! . . . And thanks for the march!

[MOZART *picks up the manuscript from the top of the fortepiano and marches happily offstage. A slight pause.* SALIERI *moves toward the audience. The lights go down around him.*]

SALIERI: [*To audience*]. Was it then—so early—that I began to have thoughts of murder? . . . Of course not: at least not in life. In art it was a different matter. I decided I would compose a huge tragic opera: something to astonish the world! And I knew my theme. I would set the legend of Danaius, who, for a monstrous crime, was chained to a rock for eternity, his head repeatedly struck by lightning! Wickedly in my head I saw Mozart in that position. . . . In reality, of course, the man was in no danger from me at all. . . . Not yet.

SCENE 8

The First Performance of
The Abduction from the Seraglio

[*The light changes, and the stage instantly turns into an eighteenth-century theater. The backdrop projection shows a line of softly gleaming chandeliers.*

The SERVANTS *bring in chairs and benches. Upon them, facing the audience and regarding it as if watching an opera, sit the* EMPEROR JOSEPH, STRACK, ROSENBERG *and* VAN SWIETEN.
Next to them: KAPELLMEISTER BONNO *and* TERESA SALIERI. *A little behind them:* CONSTANZE. *Behind her:* CITIZENS OF VIENNA.]

SALIERI: The first performance of *The Abduction from the Seraglio.* The creature's expression of manly love.

[MOZART *comes on briskly, wearing a gaudy new coat embellished with scarlet ribbons, and a new powdered wig. He struts quickly to the fortepiano, sits at it and mimes conducting.* SALIERI *sits nearby, next to his wife, and watches* MOZART *intently.*]

He himself contrived to wear for the occasion an even more vulgar coat than usual. As for the music, it matched the coat completely. For my dear pupil Katherina Cavalieri he had written quite simply the showiest Aria I'd ever heard.

[*Faintly we hear the whizzing scale passages for soprano which end the aria "Martern aller arten."*]

Ten minutes of scales and ornaments, amounting in sum to a

vast emptiness. So ridiculous was the piece, in fact—so much what might be demanded by a foolish young soprano—that I knew precisely what Mozart must have demanded in return for it.

[*The final orchestral chords of the Aria. Silence. No one moves.*]

Although engaged to be married, *he'd had her!* I knew that beyond any doubt. [*Bluntly*] The creature had had my darling girl.

[*Loudly we hear the brilliant Turkish finale of* Seraglio. *Great applause from those watching.* MOZART *jumps to his feet and acknowledges it. The* EMPEROR *rises—as do all— and gestures graciously to the "stage" in invitation.* KATHE- RINA CAVALIERI *runs on in her costume, all plumes and flounces, to renewed cheering and clapping. She curtsies to the* EMPEROR—*is kissed by* SALIERI—*presented to his wife— curtsies again to* MOZART *and, flushed with triumph, moves to one side.*

In the ensuing brief silence, CONSTANZE *rushes down from the back, wildly excited. She flings herself on* MOZART, *not even noticing the* EMPEROR.]

CONSTANZE: Oh, well done, lovey! . . . Well done, pussy-wussy! . . .

[MOZART *indicates the proximity of His Majesty.*]

Oh! . . . 'Scuse me! [*She curtsies in embarrassment.*]

MOZART: Majesty, may I present my fiancée, Fräulein Weber.

[CAVALIERI *reacts in total surprise.*]

JOSEPH: *Enchanté, Fräulein.*

CONSTANZE: Your Majesty!

MOZART: Constanze is a singer herself.

JOSEPH: Indeed?

CONSTANZE: [*Embarrassed*]. I'm not at all, Majesty. Don't be silly, Wolfgang!

JOSEPH: So, Mozart—a good effort. Decidedly that. A good effort.

MOZART: Did you really like it, Sire?

JOSEPH: I thought it was most interesting. Yes, indeed. A trifle . . . how shall one say? [*To* ROSENBERG] How shall one say, Director?

ROSENBERG: [*Subserviently*]. Too many notes, Your Majesty?

JOSEPH: Very well put. Too many notes.

MOZART: I don't understand.

JOSEPH: My dear fellow, don't take it too hard. There are in fact only so many notes the ear can hear in the course of an evening. I think I'm right in saying that, aren't I, Court Composer?

SALIERI: [*Uncomfortably*]. Well, yes, I would say yes, on the whole, yes, Majesty.

JOSEPH: There you are. It's clever. It's German. It's quality work. And there are simply too many notes. Do you see?

MOZART: There are just as many notes, Majesty, neither more nor less, as are required.

[*Pause*]

JOSEPH: Ah . . . Well—there it is! [*He goes off abruptly, followed by* ROSENBERG *and* STRACK. *The rest of the audience leaves also,* CAVALIERI *with a furious scowl.*]

MOZART: [*Nervously*]. Is he angry?

SALIERI: Not at all. He respects you for your views.

MOZART: I hope so. . . . What did you think yourself, sir? Did you care for the piece at all?

SALIERI: Yes, of course, Mozart—at its best, it is truly charming.

MOZART: And at other times?

SALIERI: [*Smoothly*]. Well, just occasionally, at other times—in Katherina's aria, for example—it was a little excessive.

MOZART: Katherina is an excessive girl. In fact, she's insatiable. . . . I mean in regard to vocal ornaments.

SALIERI: All the same, as my revered teacher the Chevalier Gluck used to say to me, one must avoid music that smells of music.

MOZART: What does that mean?

SALIERI: Music which makes one aware too much of the virtuosity of the composer.

MOZART: [*Mischievously*]. Well—I would hate to offend a *Chevalier*. Even though I myself am one.

SALIERI: Indeed?

CONSTANZE: [*Brightly*]. Oh yes! The Pope made Wolfgang a Chevalier when he was only fourteen!

SALIERI: [*Smiling*]. Extraordinary.

MOZART: They say Gluck used the name all the time. He insisted on being addressed by it.

SALIERI: And you prefer not to be?

MOZART: I think titles are absurd, in connection with music.

SALIERI: Ah. [*Slyly*] Even—"Court Composer"?

MOZART: What? . . . [*Realizing*] Ah. Oh. Ha, ha. Well! . . . That's different, of course. . . . My father's right, again. He always tells me I should padlock my mouth. . . . Actually I shouldn't speak at all!

SALIERI: [*Soothing*]. Nonsense. I'm just being what the Emperor would call *cattivo*. Won't you introduce me to your charming fiancée?

MOZART: Oh, of course! Constanze, this is Herr Salieri, the Court Composer. Fräulein Weber.

SALIERI: [*Bowing*]. Delighted, *cara Fräulein*.

CONSTANZE: [*Bobbing*]. How do you do, Excellency?

SALIERI: May I ask when you marry?

MOZART: [*Nervously*]. We have to secure my father's consent. He's an excellent man—a wonderful man—but in some ways a little stubborn.

SALIERI: Excuse me, but how old are you?

MOZART: Twenty-six.

SALIERI: Then your father's consent is scarcely indispensable.

CONSTANZE: [*To* MOZART]. You see?

MOZART: [*Uncomfortably*]. Well, no, it's not *indispensable*—of course not! . . .

SALIERI: My advice to you is to marry and be happy. You have found—it's quite obvious—*un tesoro raro!*

CONSTANZE: Ta very much.

SALIERI: [*He kisses* CONSTANZE's *hand. She is delighted.*] Good night to you both.

CONSTANZE: Good night, Excellency!

MOZART: Good night, sir. And thank you. . . . Come, Stanzerl.
[*They depart delightedly. He watches them go.*]

SALIERI: [*To audience*]. As I watched her walk away on the arm of the creature, I felt the lightning thought strike: *"Have her! Her for Katherina!"* . . . Abomination! . . . Never in my life had I entertained a notion so sinful!
[*Light change: the eighteenth century fades. The* VENTICELLI *come on merrily, as if from some celebration. One holds a bottle; the other, a glass.*]

V.I: They're married!

SALIERI: [*To them*]. What?

V.2: Mozart and Weber—married!

SALIERI: Really?

V.I: His father will be furious!

V.2: They didn't even wait for his consent!

SALIERI: Have they set up house?

V.I: Wipplingerstrasse.

V.2: Number twelve.

V.I: Not bad.

V.2: Considering they've no money.

SALIERI: Is that really true?

V.I: He's wildly extravagant.

V.2: Lives way beyond his means.

SALIERI: But he has pupils.

V.I: Only three.

SALIERI: [*To them*]. Why so few?

V.2: He's embarrassing.

V.I: Makes scenes.

V.2: Makes enemies.

V.I: Even Strack, whom he cultivates.

SALIERI: Chamberlain Strack?

V.2: Only last night.

V.1: At Kapellmeister Bonno's.

SCENE 9

Bonno's Salon

[*Instant light change. Upstage,* BONNO, *stands with a few guests.* MOZART *comes in with* STRACK. *He is high on wine, and holding a glass. The* VENTICELLI *join the scene, but still talk out of it to* SALIERI. *One of them fills* MOZART's *glass.*]

MOZART: Seven months in this city and not one job! I'm not to be tried again, is that it?

STRACK: [*Amiably*]. Of course not.

MOZART: I know what goes on, and so do you. Germany is completely in the hands of foreigners. Worthless Italians like *Kapellmeister Bonno!*

STRACK: Please! You're in the man's house!

MOZART: Court Composer *Salieri!*

STRACK: Hush!

MOZART: Did you see his last opera—*The Stolen Bucket*?! . . . Did you?

STRACK: Of course I did.

MOZART: Unbearable!

[*He sits at the fortepiano and thumps on it monotonously.*]

MOZART: [*Singing*]. Pom-pom, pom-pom, pom-pom, pom-pom! Tonic and dominant, tonic and dominant, from here to resurrection! Not one interesting modulation all night. Salieri is a musical idiot.

STRACK: Please!

v.1: [*To* SALIERI]. He'd had too much to drink.

v.2: He often has.

MOZART: Why are Italians so terrified by the slightest complexity in music? Show them one chromatic passage and they *faint!* . . . *"Oh, how sick! How morbid!"*[*Falsetto*] *Morboso!* . . . *Nervoso!* . . . *Ohimè!* . . . No wonder the music at this court is so dreary! . . . And in opera they just use the same old conventions over and over again! [*Illustrating at the keyboard*] *Tremolando* shows rage! *Sforzando* shows excitement! C Minor means gravity!—D Minor means terror! . . . Round and round like donkeys at a grindstone!

STRACK: [*Half-amused*]. Lower your voice!

MOZART: Lower your breeches. . . . That's just a joke!—
   [*Unobserved by him, Count* ROSENBERG *has entered upstage. He wears a waistcoat of dark green silk and an expression of supercilious interest.* MOZART *sees him. A pause.*]
   [*Pleasantly, to* ROSENBERG] You look like a toad . . . I mean, your waistcoat. And you were goggling like a toad.

ROSENBERG: [*Blandly*]. You would do best to retire tonight, for your own sake.

MOZART: [*Sharply*]. Salieri has fifty pupils. I have three. How am I to live? I'm a married man now! . . . Of course, I realize you don't concern yourselves with *money* in these exalted circles. All the same, did you know behind his back His Majesty is known as Kaiser Keep-it? [*He giggles naughtily.*]

STRACK: *Mozart!*
   [*He stops. All the guests upstage are watching.*]

MOZART: I shouldn't have said that, should I? . . . Forgive me. It was just a joke. Another joke! . . . I can't help myself! . . . We're all friends here, aren't we?
   [STRACK *and* ROSENBERG *glare at him. Then* STRACK *leaves abruptly, much offended.*]
   What's wrong with *him?*

ROSENBERG: Good night. [*He turns to go also.*]

MOZART: No, no, no—please! [*He grabs the* DIRECTOR's *arm.*]
Your hand please, first!

[*Unwillingly,* ROSENBERG *gives him his hand.* MOZART
kisses it.]

[*Humbly*] Give me a post, sir.

ROSENBERG: That is not in my power, Mozart.

MOZART: The Princess Elizabeth is looking for an instructor. One
word from you could secure it for me.

ROSENBERG: I regret that is solely in the recommendation of Court
Composer Salieri. [*He disengages himself.*]

MOZART: Do you know I am better than any musician in
Vienna? . . . Do you?

[ROSENBERG *leaves.* MOZART *calls after him.*]

Italians! . . . I'm *sick* of them! . . . Italians *everywhere!*

[*He runs at the upstage guests in mock aggression. Old*
BONNO *shepherds them offstage in alarm. The* VENTICELLI
leave hurriedly, another way. MOZART *is left alone—save of
course for* SALIERI *standing out of the scene, to one side.*
MOZART *looks about him, then suddenly giggles to himself
like a child, and starts to sing with bravado, to the tune that
one day will be that of* "Là ci darem lo mano" *in his* Don
Giovanni.]

MOZART: [*Singing*]. "The girl who doesn't love me—the girl who
doesn't love me—the girl who doesn't love me—can lick my
arse instead!" . . .

[*But suddenly he strikes his own head fiercely in self-rebuke,
and dashes offstage.*]

SALIERI: [*Watching him go, to audience*]. Barely one month later
that thought of revenge became more than thought.

SCENE 10

The Waldstädten Library

[*Two simultaneous shouts bring up the lights. Against the handsome wallpaper stand three masked figures:* CON-STANZE, *flanked on either side by the* VENTICELLI. *All three are guests at a party, and are playing a game of forfeits.*
Two SERVANTS *stand frozen, holding the large wing chair between them. Two more hold the big table of sweetmeats.*]

V.1: Forfeit! . . . Forfeit! . . .

V.2: Forfeit, Stanzerl! You've got to forfeit!

CONSTANZE: I won't.

V.1: You have to.

V.2: It's the game.

[*The* SERVANTS *unfreeze and set down the furniture.* SALIERI *moves to the wing chair and sits.*]

SALIERI: [*To audience*]. Once again—believe it or not—I was in the same concealing chair in the Baroness's library [*Taking a cup from the little table*] and consuming the same delicious dessert.

V.1: You lost—now there's the penalty!

SALIERI: [*To audience*]. A party celebrating the New Year's Eve. I was on my own—my dear spouse, Teresa, visiting her parents in Italy.

CONSTANZE: Well, *what?* . . . What is it?

[VENTICELLO ONE *snatches up an old-fashioned round ruler from off the fortepiano.*]

V.1: I want to measure your calves.

CONSTANZE: Oooo!

V.1: Well?

CONSTANZE: Definitely not. You cheeky bugger!

V.1: Now come on!

v.2: You've got to let him, Stanzerl. All's fair in love and forfeits.

CONSTANZE: No, it isn't—so you can both buzz off!

v.1: If you don't let me, you won't be allowed to play again.

CONSTANZE: Well, choose something else.

v.2: I've chosen that! Now get up on the table. Quick, quick! *Allez-oop!* [*Gleefully he shifts the plates of sweetmeats to the forte-piano.*]

CONSTANZE: Quick, then! . . . Before anyone sees!

[*The two masked men lift the shrieking masked girl up onto the table.*]

v.1: Hold her, Friedrich.

CONSTANZE: I don't have to be held, thank you!

v.2: Yes, you do—that's part of the penalty.

[*He holds her ankles firmly, while* VENTICELLO ONE *thrusts the ruler under her skirts and measures her legs. Excitedly,* SALIERI *reverses his position so that he can kneel in the wing chair and watch.* CONSTANZE *giggles delightedly, then becomes outraged—or pretends to be.*]

CONSTANZE: Stop it! . . . Stop that! That's quite enough of that!

[*She bends down and tries to slap him.*]

v.1: Seventeen inches—knee to ankle!

v.2: Let me do it! You hold her.

CONSTANZE: That's not fair!

v.1: Yes, it is. You lost to me too.

CONSTANZE: It's been done now! Let me *down!*

v.2: Hold her, Karl.

CONSTANZE: No! . . .

[VENTICELLO ONE *holds her ankles.* VENTICELLO TWO *thrusts his head entirely under her skirts. She squeals.*]

No—stop it! . . . No! . . .

[*In the middle of this undignified scene,* MOZART *comes rushing on, also masked.*]

MOZART: [*Outraged*]. Constanze!

[*They freeze.* SALIERI *ducks back down and sits hidden in the chair.*]

Gentlemen, if you please.

CONSTANZE: It's only a game, Wolferl! . . .

V.I: We meant no harm, 'pon my word.

MOZART: [*Stiffly*]. Come down off that table, please.

[*They hand her down.*]

Thank you. We'll see you later.

V.2: Now look, Mozart, don't be pompous—

MOZART: Please excuse us now.

[*They go. The little man is very angry. He tears off his mask.*]

[*To* CONSTANZE] Do you realize what you've done?

CONSTANZE: No, what? . . . [*Flustered, she busies herself restoring the plates of sweetmeats to the table.*]

MOZART: Just lost your reputation, that's all! You're now a loose girl.

CONSTANZE: Don't be so stupid. [*She, too, removes her mask.*]

MOZART: You are a married woman, for God's sake!

CONSTANZE: And what of it?

MOZART: A young wife does not allow her legs to be handled in public. Couldn't you at least have measured your own ugly legs?

CONSTANZE: *What?*

MOZART: [*Raising his voice*]. Do you know what you've done?!. . . . You've shamed me, that's all! *Shamed* me!

CONSTANZE: Oh, don't be so ridiculous!

MOZART: Shamed me—in front of *them!*

CONSTANZE: [*Suddenly furious*]. *You?* Shamed *you?* . . . That's a laugh! If there's any shame around, lovey, it's *mine!*

MOZART: What do you mean?

CONSTANZE: You've only had every pupil who ever came to you.

MOZART: That's not true.

CONSTANZE: Every single female pupil!

MOZART: Name them! *Name them!*

CONSTANZE: The Aurnhammer girl! The Rumbeck girl! Katherina
Cavalieri—that sly little whore! *She* wasn't even your pupil—
she was Salieri's. Which actually, my dear, may be why he has
hundreds and you have none. He doesn't drag them into bed!

MOZART: Of course he doesn't! He can't get it up, that's why! . . .
Have you heard his music? That's the sound of someone who
can't get it up! At least *I* can do *that!*

CONSTANZE: I'm sick of you!

MOZART: No one ever said I couldn't do *that!*

CONSTANZE: [*Bursting into tears*]. I don't give a fart! I hate you! I
hate you for ever and ever—I hate you! [*A tiny pause. She
weeps.*]

MOZART: [*Helplessly*]. Oh, Stanzerl, don't cry. Please don't cry. . . .
I can't bear it when you cry. I just didn't want you to look cheap
in people's eyes, that's all. Here! [*He snatches up the ruler.*] Beat
me. Beat me. . . . I'm your slave. Stanzi marini. Stanzi marini
bini gini. I'll just stand here like a little lamb and bear your
strokes. Here. Do it. . . . *Batti.*

CONSTANZE: No.

MOZART: *Batti, batti. Mio tesoro!*

CONSTANZE: No!

MOZART: Stanzerly wanzerly piggly poo!

CONSTANZE: Stop it.

MOZART: Stanzy wanzy had a fit. Shit her stays and made them
split!

  [*She giggles despite herself.*]

CONSTANZE: Stop it.

MOZART: When they took away her skirt, Stanzy wanzy ate the
dirt!

CONSTANZE: Stop it now! [*She snatches the ruler and gives him a
whack with it. He yowls playfully.*]

MOZART: Oooo! Oooo! Oooo! Do it again! Do it again! I cast
myself at your stinking feet, Madonna!

[*He does so. She whacks him some more as he crouches, but always lightly, scarcely looking at him, divided between tears and laughter.* MOZART *drums his feet with pleasure.*]

Ow! . . . Ow! . . . Ow!

[*And then suddenly* SALIERI, *unable to bear another second, cries out involuntarily.*]

SALIERI: *Ah!!!*

[*The young couple freezes.* SALIERI, *discovered, hastily converts his noise of disgust into a yawn, and stretches as if waking up from a nap. He peers out of the wing chair.*]

Good evening.

CONSTANZE: [*Embarrassed*]. Excellency. . . .

MOZART: How long have you been there?

SALIERI: I was asleep until a second ago. Are you two quarreling?

MOZART: No, of course not.

CONSTANZE: Yes, we are. He's been very irritating.

SALIERI: [*Rising*]. *Caro Herr,* tonight is the time for New Year resolutions. Irritating lovely ladies cannot surely be one of ours. May I suggest you bring us each a *sorbetto* from the dining room?

MOZART: But why don't we all go to the table?

CONSTANZE: Herr Salieri is quite right. Bring them here—it'll be your punishment.

MOZART: Stanzi!

SALIERI: Come now, I can keep your wife company. There cannot be a better peace offering than a *sorbetto* of aniseed.

CONSTANZE: I prefer tangerine.

SALIERI: Very well, tangerine. [*Greedily*] But if you could possibly manage aniseed for me, I'd be deeply obliged. . . . So the New Year can begin coolly for all three of us.

[*A pause.* MOZART *hesitates—and then bows.*]

MOZART: I'm honored, *Signore,* of course. And then I'll play you at billiards. What do you say?

SALIERI: I'm afraid I don't play.

MOZART: [*With surprise*]. You don't?

CONSTANZE: Wolferl would rather play at billiards than anything. He's very good at it.

MOZART: I'm the best! I may nod occasionally at composing, but at billiards—never!

SALIERI: A virtuoso of the cue.

MOZART: Exactly! It's a virtuoso's game! . . . [*He snatches up the ruler and treats it as if it were a cue.*] I think I shall write a Grand Fantasia for Billiard Balls! Trills. Accacciaturas! Whole arpeggios in ivory! Then I'll play it myself in public! . . . It'll have to be *me* because none of those Italian charlatans like Clementi will be able to get his fingers round the cue!

[*He gives a swanky flourish of the hand and starts to strut off stage, then suddenly realizes what he has just said and stops.*] *Scusate, Signore!*

[SALIERI *gives him a cold nod.* MOZART *leaves, embarrassed.*]

CONSTANZE: He's a love, really.

SALIERI: And lucky too, in you. You are, if I may say so, an astonishing creature.

CONSTANZE: Me? . . . Ta very much.

SALIERI: On the other hand, your husband does not appear to be so thriving.

CONSTANZE: [*Seizing her opportunity*]. We're desperate, sir.

SALIERI: What?

CONSTANZE: We've no money and no prospects of any. That's the truth.

SALIERI: I don't understand. He gives many public concerts.

CONSTANZE: They don't pay enough. What he needs is pupils. Illustrious pupils. His father calls us spendthrifts, but that's unfair. I manage as well as anyone could. There's simply not enough. Don't tell him I talked to you, please.

SALIERI: [*Intimately*]. This is solely between us. How can I help?

CONSTANZE: My husband needs security, sir. If only he could find regular employment, everything would be all right. Is there nothing at court?

SALIERI: Not at the moment.

CONSTANZE: [*Harder*]. The Princess Elizabeth needs a tutor.

SALIERI: Really? I hadn't heard.

CONSTANZE: One word from you and the post would be his. Other pupils would follow at once.

SALIERI: [*Looking off*]. He's coming back.

CONSTANZE: Please . . . please, Excellency. You can't imagine what a difference it would make.

SALIERI: We can't speak of it now.

CONSTANZE: When, then? Oh, please!

SALIERI: Can you come and see me tomorrow? Alone?

CONSTANZE: I can't do that.

SALIERI: I'm a married man.

CONSTANZE: All the same.

SALIERI: When does he work?

CONSTANZE: Afternoons.

SALIERI: Then come at three.

CONSTANZE: I can't possibly!

SALIERI: Yes or no? . . . In his interests? . . .

[*A pause. Constanze hesitates—opens her mouth—then abruptly runs off. The curtains descend on the Light Box.*]

SALIERI: [*To audience*]. So: I'd done it! Spoken aloud! Invited her! . . . What of that vow made in church? Fidelity—virtue— all of that? I couldn't think of that now!

[SERVANTS *remove the Waldstädten furniture. Others replace it with two small gilded chairs, center, quite close together. Others, again surreptitiously, bring in the old dressing gown and cap which* SALIERI *discarded before Scene 3, placing them on the fortepiano.*]

SCENE II

Salieri's Apartment

[*On the curtains are thrown projections of long windows.*]

SALIERI: Next afternoon I waited in a fever. Would she come? I had
no idea. And if she did, how would I behave? Was I actually
going to seduce a young wife of two months standing? . . . Part
of me—much of me—wanted it, badly. *Badly.* Yes, badly was
the word!

[*The clock strikes three. On the second stroke, the bell
sounds. He rises excitedly.*]

There she was! On the stroke! She'd come. . . . She'd *come!*

[*Enter from the right the* COOK, *as fat, but forty years
younger. He proudly carries a plate piled with brandied
chestnuts.* SALIERI *takes them from him nervously, nodding
with approval, and sets them on the table.*]

[*To the* COOK] *Grazie. Grazie tanti. . . . Via, via, via!*

[*The* COOK *bows as* SALIERI *dismisses him, and goes out the
same way, smirking suggestively. The* VALET *comes in from
the left—he is also forty years younger—and behind him*
CONSTANZE, *wearing a pretty hat and carrying a portfolio.*]

SALIERI: *Signora!*

CONSTANZE: [*Curtsying*]. Excellency.

SALIERI: *Benvenuta.* [*To* VALET *in dismissal*] *Grazie.*

[*The* VALET *goes.*]

Well. You have come.

CONSTANZE: I should not have done. My husband would be frantic
if he knew. He's a very jealous man.

SALIERI: Are you a jealous woman?

CONSTANZE: Why do you ask?

SALIERI: It's not a passion I understand. . . . You're looking even
prettier than you were last night, if I may say so.

CONSTANZE: Ta very much! . . . I brought you some manuscripts by Wolfgang. When you see them, you'll understand how right he is for a royal appointment. Will you look at them, please, while I wait?

SALIERI: You mean now?

CONSTANZE: Yes. I have to take them back with me. He'll miss them otherwise. He doesn't make copies. These are all the originals.

SALIERI: Sit down. Let me offer you something special.

CONSTANZE: [*Sitting*]. What's that?

SALIERI: [*Producing the box*]. *Capezzoli di Venere*. Nipples of Venus. Roman chestnuts in brandied sugar.

CONSTANZE: No, thank you.

SALIERI: Do try. My cook made them especially for you.

CONSTANZE: Me?

SALIERI: Yes. They're quite rare.

CONSTANZE: Well then, I'd better, hadn't I? Just one. . . . Ta very much. [*She takes one and puts it in her mouth. The taste amazes her.*] Oh! . . . Oh! . . . Oh! . . . They're *delish*!

SALIERI: [*Lustfully watching her eat*]. Aren't they?

CONSTANZE: Mmmmm!

SALIERI: Have another.

CONSTANZE: [*Taking two more*]. I couldn't possibly.
  [*Carefully he moves round behind her, and seats himself on the chair next to her.*]

SALIERI: I think you're the most generous girl in the world.

CONSTANZE: Generous?

SALIERI: It's my word for you. I thought last night that Constanze is altogether too stiff a name for that girl. I shall rechristen her Generosa. *La Generosa*. Then I'll write a glorious song for her under that title and she'll sing it, just for me.

CONSTANZE: [*Smiling*]. I am much out of practice, sir.

SALIERI: *La Generosa*. [*He leans a little toward her.*] Don't tell me it's going to prove inaccurate, my name for you.

CONSTANZE: [*Coolly*]. What name do you give your wife, Excellency?

SALIERI: [*Equally coolly*]. I'm not an excellency, and I call my wife Signora Salieri. If I named her anything else, it would be *La Statua*. She is a very upright lady.

CONSTANZE: Is she here now? I'd like to meet her.

SALIERI: Alas, no. At the moment she's visiting her mother in Verona. [*She starts very slightly out of her chair.* SALIERI *gently restrains her.*]

SALIERI: Constanze: tomorrow evening I dine with the Emperor. One word from me recommending your husband as tutor to the Princess Elizabeth, and that invaluable post is his. Believe me, when I speak to His Majesty in matters musical, no one contradicts me.

CONSTANZE: I believe you.

SALIERI: *Bene.* [*Still sitting, he takes his* mouchoir *and delicately wipes her mouth with it.*] Surely service of that sort deserves a little recompense in return?

CONSTANZE: How little?

[*Slight pause*]

SALIERI: The size of a kiss.

[*Slight pause*]

CONSTANZE: Just one?

[*Slight pause*]

SALIERI: If one seems fair to you.

[*She looks at him—then kisses him lightly on the mouth. Longer pause.*]

Does it?

[*She gives him a longer kiss. He touches her with his hand. She breaks off.*]

CONSTANZE: I fancy that's fairness enough.

[*Pause*]

SALIERI: [*Carefully*]. A pity . . . It's somewhat small pay, to secure a post every musician in Vienna is hoping for.

CONSTANZE: What do you mean?

SALIERI: Is it not clear?

CONSTANZE: No. Not at all.

SALIERI: Another pity . . . A thousand pities.

[*Pause*]

CONSTANZE: I don't believe it . . . I just don't believe it!

SALIERI: What?

CONSTANZE: What you've just said.

SALIERI: [*Hastily*]. I said nothing. What did I say?

[CONSTANZE *gets up and* SALIERI *rises in panic*.]

CONSTANZE: Oh, I'm going! . . . I'm getting out of this!

SALIERI: Constanze . . .

CONSTANZE: Let me pass, please.

SALIERI: Constanze, listen to me! I'm a clumsy man. You think me sophisticated—I'm not at all. Take a true look. I've no cunning. I live on ink and sweetmeats. I never see women at all. . . . When I met you last night, I envied Mozart from the depths of my soul. Out of that envy came stupid thoughts. For one silly second I dared imagine that, out of the vast store you obviously possess, you might spare me one coin of tenderness your rich husband does not need—and inspire me also.

[*Pause. She laughs.*]

I amuse.

CONSTANZE: Mozart was right. You're wicked.

SALIERI: He said that?

CONSTANZE: "All Italians are performers," he said. "Be very careful with that one." Meaning you. He was being comic, of course.

SALIERI: Yes.

[*Abruptly he turns his back on her.*]

CONSTANZE: But not that comic, actually. I mean, you're acting a pretty obvious role, aren't you, dear? A small-town boy, and all the time as clever as cutlets! . . . [*Mock tender*] Ah! You are sulking? *Are* you? . . . When Mozart sulks, I smack his botty.

He rather likes it. Do you want me to scold you a bit and smack your botty too? [*She hits him lightly with the portfolio. He turns in a fury.*]

SALIERI: How dare you?! . . . *You silly, common girl!*

[*A dreadful silence*]

[*Icy*] Forgive me. Let us confine our talk to your husband. He is a brilliant keyboard player, no question. However, the Princess Elizabeth also requires a tutor in vocal music. I am not convinced he is the man for that. I would like to look at the pieces you've brought, and decide if he is mature enough. I will study them overnight—and you will study my proposal. Not to be vague, that is the price. [*He extends his hand for the portfolio, and she surrenders it.*] Good afternoon.

[*He turns from her and places it on a chair. She lingers—tries to speak—cannot—and goes out quickly.*]

SCENE 12

The Same

[SALIERI *turns in a ferment to the audience.*]

SALIERI: Fiasco! . . . Fiasco! . . . The sordidness of it! The sheer sweating sordidness! . . . Worse than if I'd actually done it! . . . To be that much in sin and feel so *ridiculous* as well! [*Crying out*] Nobile, nobile Salieri! . . . What had he done to me, this Mozart? Before he came, did I behave like this? Toy with adultery? Blackmail women? It was all going—slipping—growing rotten . . . because of *him!*

[*He moves upstage in a fever—reaches out to take the portfolio on the chair—but as if fearful of what he might find inside it, he withdraws his hand and sits instead beside it. A*] *pause. He contemplates the music lying there as if it were a great confection he is dying to eat, but dare not. Then suddenly he snatches at it—tears the ribbon—opens the case and stares greedily at the manuscripts within.*

Music sounds instantly, faintly, in the theater, as his eye falls on the first page. It is the opening of the Twenty-ninth Symphony, in A major. Over the music, reading it.]

She had said that these were his original scores. First and only drafts of the music. Yet they looked like fair copies. They showed no corrections of any kind. It was puzzling—then suddenly alarming.

[*He looks up from the manuscript at the audience: the music abruptly stops.*]

What was evident was that Mozart was simply transcribing music completely finished in his head. And finished as most music is never finished.

[*He resumes looking at the music. Immediately the Sinfonia Concertante for Violin and Viola sounds.*]

Displace one note and there would be diminishment. Displace one phrase and the structure would fall.

[*He looks up again: the music breaks off.*]

Here again—only now in abundance—were the same sounds I'd heard in the library.

[*He resumes reading, and the music also resumes: a ravishing phrase from the slow movement of the Concerto for Flute and Harp.*]

The same crushed harmonies—glancing collisions—agonizing delights.

[*He looks up again. The music stops.*]

The truth was clear. That Serenade had been no accident.

[*Very low, in the theater, a faint thundery sound is heard accumulating, like a distant sea.*]

I was staring through the cage of those meticulous ink strokes at—an Absolute Beauty!

[*He rises to his feet, holding the portfolio. And out of the thundery roar writhes and rises the clear sound of a soprano, singing the Kyrie from the C minor Mass. The accretion of noise around her voice falls away—it is suddenly clear and bright, then clearer and brighter. The light also grows bright, too bright: burning white, then scalding white!* SALIERI *stands in the downpour of it, in the flood of the music, which is growing ever louder—filling the theater—as the soprano yields to the full chorus singing fortissimo its massive counterpoint.*

This is by far the loudest sound the audience has yet heard. SALIERI *staggers toward us, holding the manuscripts in his hand, like a man caught in a tumbling and violent sea. Finally the drums crash in below.* SALIERI *throws down the portfolio of manuscripts—and falls senseless to the ground. At the same second the music explodes into a long, echoing, distorted boom, signifying some dreadful annihilation. The sound remains suspended over the prone figure in a menacing continuum—no longer music at all. Then it dies away, and there is only silence.*

The light fades again.

A long pause.

SALIERI *is quite still, lying among the manuscripts. Finally the clock sounds: seven times.* SALIERI *stirs as it does. Slowly he raises his head and looks up. And now—quietly at first—he addresses his God.*]

SALIERI: *Capisco!* I know my fate. Now for the first time I feel my emptiness as Adam felt his nakedness. . . . [*Slowly he rises to his feet.*] Tonight at an inn somewhere in this city stands a giggling child who can put on paper, without actually setting down his billiard cue, casual notes which turn my most considered ones into lifeless scratches. *Grazie, Signore!* You gave me the desire to serve You—which most men do not have—then saw to it the service was shameful in the ears of the server. *Grazie!* You gave me the desire to praise You—which most men do not feel—then made me mute. *Grazie tante!* You put into me the perception of the Incomparable—which most men never know!—then ensured that I would know myself forever mediocre. [*His voice gains power.*]

Why? . . . What is my fault? . . . Until this day I have pursued virtue with rigor. I have labored long hours to relieve my fellow men. I have worked and worked the talent You allowed me. [*Calling up*] *You know how hard I've worked!* Solely that in the end, in the practice of the art, which alone makes the world comprehensible to me, I might hear Your Voice! And now I do hear it—and it says only one name: MOZART! . . . Spiteful, sniggering, conceited, infantine Mozart—who has never worked one minute to help another man! Shit-talking Mozart, with his botty-smacking wife! *Him* You have chosen to be Your sole conduit! And *my* only reward—my sublime privilege—is to be the sole man alive in this time who shall clearly recognize Your Incarnation! [*Savagely*] *Grazie e grazie ancora!*

[*He hurls the portfolio into a corner.*]

So be it! From this time we are enemies, You and I! I'll not accept it from you—*do you hear? . . .* They say God is not mocked. I tell You, *Man* is not mocked! . . . I am not mocked! . . . They say the spirit bloweth where it listeth: I tell You *no!* It must list to virtue or not blow at all! [*Yelling*] *Dio ingiusto*—You are the Enemy! I name Thee now—*Nemico Eterno!* And this I swear: To my last breath I shall *block* You on earth, as far as I am able! [*He glares up at God. To audience*] What use, after all, is Man, if not to teach God His lessons?

[*He slips off his powdered wig, crosses to the fortepiano and takes from its lid where they lie the old dressing gown and cap which he discarded when he conducted us back to the eighteenth century. He slips these on. As he does this, he speaks again in the voice of an old man. It is 1823 again.*]

Before I tell you what happened next—God's answer to me

and indeed Constanze's—and all the horrors that followed—let
me stop. The bladder, being a human appendage, is not something you need concern yourselves with yet. I being alive,
though barely, am at its constant call. It is now one hour before
dawn—when I must dismiss us both. When I return, I'll tell you
about the war I fought with God through His preferred Creature—Mozart, named *Amadeus*. In the waging of which, of
course, the Creature had to be destroyed.

[*He bows to the audience, reaches out to snatch up a pas-
try—then, unexpectedly, puts it back on the plate in sudden
self-disgust, and slowly hobbles off stage. The manuscripts
lie where he spilled them in his fall. As he disappears, the
house lights slowly come up.*]

END OF ACT ONE

ACT TWO

SCENE I

Salieri's Apartment

[*The lights go down in the theater as* SALIERI *returns as the old man.*]

SALIERI: I have been listening to the cats in the courtyard. They are all singing Rossini. It is obvious that cats have declined as badly as composers. Domenico Scarlatti owned one which would actually stroll across the keyboard and pick out passable subjects for fugue. But that was a Spanish cat of the Enlightenment. It appreciated counterpoint. Nowadays all cats appreciate is coloratura. Like the rest of the public.

[*He comes downstage and addresses the audience directly.*]

This is now the very last hour of my life. You must understand me. Not forgive. I do not seek forgiveness. I was a good man, as the world calls good. What use was it to me? Goodness could not make me a good composer! . . . Was Mozart "good?" Goodness is nothing in the furnace of art.

[*Pause*]

On that dreadful Night of the Manuscripts my life acquired a terrible and thrilling purpose. The blocking of God in one of His purest manifestations. I had the power. God needed Mozart to let Himself into the world. And Mozart needed me to get him worldly advancement. So it would be a battle to the end—and Mozart was the battleground.

[*Pause*]

One thing I knew of Him. He was a cunning Enemy. Witness the fact that in blocking Him in the world I was also given the satisfaction of obstructing a disliked human rival. I wonder which of *you* will refuse that chance if it is offered.

[*He regards the audience maliciously and takes off the dressing gown and cap. She wears a hat and shawl.*]

I felt the danger at once, as soon as I'd spoken my challenge. How would He answer? Would He strike me dead for my impiety? Don't laugh. I was not a sophisticate of the salons. I was a small-town Catholic, full of dread!

[*He puts on the powdered wig again and speaks again in his younger voice. We are back again in the eighteenth century.*]

The first thing that happened, barely one hour later—

[*The doorbell sounds.* CONSTANZE *comes in, followed by a helpless* VALET.]

Suddenly Constanze was back. [*In surprise*] At ten o'clock at night! . . .

Signora!

CONSTANZE: [*Stiffly*]. My husband is at a soiree of Baron van Swieten. A concert of Sebastian Bach. He didn't think I would enjoy it.

SALIERI: I see. [*Curtly, to the goggling* VALET] I'll ring if we require anything. Thank you.

[*The* VALET *goes out. Slight pause.*]

CONSTANZE: [*Flatly*]. Where do we go, then?

SALIERI: What?

CONSTANZE: Do we do it in here? . . . Why not?

[*She sits, still wearing her hat, in one of the little gilded upright chairs. Deliberately she loosens the strings of her bodice, so that one can just see the tops of her breasts, hitches up her silk skirts above the knees, so that one can also just see the flesh above the tops of the stockings, spreads her legs and regards him with an open stare.*]

[*Speaking quietly*] Well? . . . Let's get on with it.

[*For a second* SALIERI *returns the stare, then looks suddenly away.*]

SALIERI: [*Stiffly*]. Your manuscripts are there. Please take them and go. Now. At once.

[*Pause*]

CONSTANZE: You shit. [*She jumps up and snatches the portfolio.*]

SALIERI: *Via! Don't return!*

CONSTANZE: You rotten shit!

[*Suddenly she runs at him, trying furiously to hit at his face. He grabs her arms, shakes her violently and hurls her on the floor.*]

SALIERI: *Via!*

[*She freezes, staring up at him in hate.*]

[*Calling to audience*] You see how it was! I would have liked her—oh, yes, just then more than ever! But I wanted nothing petty! . . . My quarrel now wasn't with Mozart—it was *through* him! Through him to *God,* who loved him so. [*Scornfully*] *Amadeus! . . . Amadeus! . . .*

[CONSTANZE *picks herself up and runs from the room. Pause. He calms himself, going to the table and selecting a "Nipple of Venus" to eat.*]

The next day, when Katherina Cavalieri came for her lesson, I made the same halting speech about "coins of tenderness," and I dubbed the girl *La Generosa.* I regret that my invention in love, as in art, has always been limited. Fortunately, Katherina found it sufficient. She consumed twenty "Nipples of Venus"—kissed me with brandied breath—and slipped easily into my bed.

[KATHERINA *comes in languidly, half undressed, as if from his bedroom. He embraces her, and helps slyly to adjust her peignoir.*]

She remained there as my mistress for many years behind my good wife's back—and I soon erased in sweat the sense of his little body, the Creature's, preceding me.

[*The girl gives him a radiant smile, and ambles off.*]
So much for my vow of sexual virtue. [*Slight pause*] The same evening I went to the Palace and resigned from all my committees to help the lot of poor musicians. So much for my vow of social virtue.

[*Light change*]

Then I went to the Emperor and recommended a man of no talent whatever to instruct the Princess Elizabeth.

S C E N E 2

The Palace of Schönbrunn

[*The* EMPEROR *stands before the vast fireplace, between the golden mirrors.*]

JOSEPH: Herr Sommer. A dull man, surely? What of Mozart?

SALIERI: Majesty, I cannot with a clear conscience recommend Mozart to teach royalty. One hears too many stories.

JOSEPH: They may be just gossip.

SALIERI: One of them, I regret, relates to a protégée of my own. A very young singer.

JOSEPH: *Charmant!*

SALIERI: Not pleasant, Majesty, but true.

JOSEPH: I see. . . . Let it be Herr Sommer, then. [*He walks down onto the main stage.*] I daresay he can't do much harm. To be frank, no one can do much harm musically to the Princess Elizabeth. [*He strolls away to one side.*]

[MOZART *enters from the other side, downstage. He wears a more natural-looking wig from now on—one indeed intended to represent his own hair of light chestnut, full and gathered at the back with ribbon.*]

SALIERI: [*To audience*]. Mozart certainly did not suspect me. The Emperor announced the appointment in his usual way—

JOSEPH: [*Pausing*]. Well—there it is. [*He goes off.*]

SALIERI: And I commiserated with the loser.

[MOZART *turns and stares bleakly out front.* SALIERI *shakes his hand.*]

MOZART: [*Bitterly*]. It's my own fault. My father always writes I should be more obedient. *Know my place!* . . . He'll send me sixteen lectures when he hears of this!

[MOZART *goes slowly up to the fortepiano. Lights lower.*]

SALIERI: [*Watching him, to audience*]. It was a most serious loss as far as *Mozart* was concerned.

SCENE 3

Vienna, and Glimpses of Opera Houses

[*The* VENTICELLI *glide on.*]

V.1: His list of pupils hardly moves.

V.2: Six at most.

V.1: And now a child to keep!

V.2: A boy.

SALIERI: Poor fellow. [*To audience*] I by contrast prospered. This is the extraordinary truth. If I had expected fury from God, none came. *None!* . . . Instead—incredibly—in '84 and '85 I came to be regarded as infinitely the superior composer. And this despite the fact that these were the two years in which Mozart wrote his best keyboard concerti and his string quartets.

[*The* VENTICELLI *stand on either side of* SALIERI. MOZART *sits at the fortepiano.*]

V.1: Haydn calls the quartets unsurpassed.

SALIERI: They were, but no one heard them.

V.2: Van Swieten calls the concerti sublime.

SALIERI: They were, but no one noticed.

> [MOZART *plays and conducts from the keyboard. Faintly we hear the Rondo from the Piano Concerto in A major, K. 488.*]

[*Over this*] The Viennese greeted each concerto with the squeals of pleasure they usually reserved for a new style of bonnet. Each was played once—then totally forgotten! . . . By contrast, my operas were played everywhere and saluted by everyone! . . . I composed a *Semiramide* for Munich.

V.1: Rapturously received!

V.2: People *faint* with pleasure!

> [*In the Light Box is seen the interior of a brilliantly colored opera house, and an audience standing up, applauding vigorously.* SALIERI, *flanked by the* VENTICELLI, *turns upstage and bows to it. Mozart's concert can barely be heard through the din.*]

SALIERI: I wrote a comic opera for Vienna. *La Grotta di Trofonio.*

V.1: The talk of the city!

V.2: The cafés are buzzing!

> [*Another opera house interior is lit up. Another audience claps vigorously. Again* SALIERI *bows to it.*]

SALIERI: [*To audience*]. I finally finished my tragic opera *Danaius,* and produced it in Paris.

V.1: Stupendous reception!

V.2: The plaudits shake the roof!

V.1: Your name sounds throughout the Empire!

V.2: Throughout all Europe!

> [*Yet another opera house and another excited audience.* SALIERI *bows a third time. Even the* VENTICELLI *now applaud him. Mozart's concert stops. He rises from the keyboard and, while* SALIERI *speaks, stumps directly through the scene and leaves the stage.*]

SALIERI: [*To audience*]. It was incomprehensible. Almost as if I were being pushed deliberately from triumph to triumph! . . . I filled my head with golden opinions—yes, and this house with golden furniture!

SCENE 4

Salieri's Apartment

[*The stage turns gold.*
SERVANTS *come on carrying golden chairs upholstered in golden brocade. They place these all over the wooden floor. The* VALET *appears—a little older—divests* SALIERI *of his sober coat and clothes him instead in another one with gold facings. The* COOK—*also, of course, a little older—brings in a golden cake-stand piled with more elaborate cakes.*]

SALIERI: My own taste was for plain things—but I *denied* it! The successful lived with gold, and so would I! . . . I grew confident. I grew resplendent. I gave salons and soirees, and worshiped the season round at the altar of sophistication!

[*He sits at ease in his salon. The* VENTICELLI *sit with him, one on either side.*]

V.1: Mozart heard your comedy last night.

V.2: He spoke of it to the Princess Lichnowsky.

V.1: He said you should be made to clean up your own mess.

SALIERI: [*Taking snuff*]. *Really?* What charmers these Salzburgers are!

V.2: People are outraged by him.

V.1: He empties drawing rooms. Now van Swieten is angry with him.

[*The* VENTICELLI *laugh maliciously.*]

SALIERI: Lord Fugue? . . . I thought he was the Baron's little pet.

V.2: Mozart has asked leave to write an Italian opera.

SALIERI: [To audience]. Italian opera! Threat! My kingdom!

V.1: And the Baron is scandalized.

SALIERI: But why? What's the subject?

[VAN SWIETEN comes on quickly from upstage.]

VAN SWIETEN: Figaro! . . . The Marriage of Figaro! That disgrace-
ful play of Beaumarchais!

[At a discreet sign of dismissal from SALIERI, the VENTICELLI
slip away. VAN SWIETEN joins SALIERI, and sits on one of the
gold chairs.]

VAN SWIETEN: [To SALIERI]. That's all he can find to waste his talent on: a vulgar farce! Noblemen lusting after chambermaids!
Their wives dressing up in stupid disguises anyone could pene-
trate in a second! . . . When I reproved him, he said I reminded
him of his father! . . . I simply cannot imagine why Mozart
should want to set that rubbish to music!

[MOZART enters quickly from upstage, accompanied by
STRACK. They join SALIERI and VAN SWIETEN.]

MOZART: Because I want to do a piece about real people, Baron!
And I want to set it in a real place! A boudoir! Because that to
me is the most exciting place on earth! Underclothes on the
floor! Sheets still warm from a woman's body! Even a pisspot
brimming under the bed!

VAN SWIETEN: [Outraged]. Mozart!

MOZART: I want life, Baron. Not boring legends!

STRACK: [Sitting]. Herr Salieri's recent Danaius was a legend, and
that did not bore the French.

MOZART: It is impossible to bore the French—except with real life!

VAN SWIETEN: I had assumed, now that you had joined our Brotherhood of Masons, you would choose more elevated themes.

MOZART: [Impatiently]. Oh, elevated! Elevated! . . . The only thing
a man should elevate is his doodle.

VAN SWIETEN: You are provoking, sir! Has everything to be a joke with you?

MOZART: [*Desperate*]. Excuse the language, Baron, but really! . . . How can we go on forever with these gods and heroes?

VAN SWIETEN: [*Passionately*]. Because they *go* on forever—that's why! They represent the eternal in us. Opera is here to ennoble us, Mozart—you and me just as well as the Emperor. It is an aggrandizing art! It celebrates the eternal in Man and ignores the ephemeral. The goddess in Woman and not the laundress.

STRACK: Well said, sir. Exactly!

MOZART: [*Imitating his drawl*]. Oh, well said, yes, well said! Exactly! [*To all of them*] I don't understand you! You're all up on perches, but it doesn't hide your arseholes! You don't give a shit about gods and heroes! If you are honest—each one of you—which of you isn't more at home with his hairdresser than Hercules? Or Horatius?

[*To* SALIERI] Or your stupid Danaius, come to that! Or *mine— mine! Idomeneo, King of Crete!* All those anguished antiques! They're all bores! Bores, bores, bores! [*Suddenly he springs up onto a chair, like an orator. Declaring it*] All serious operas written this century are boring!

[*They turn and look at him in shocked amazement. A pause. He gives a little giggle, and then jumps down again.*]

Look at us! Four gaping mouths. What a perfect quartet! I'd love to write it—just this second of time, this *now*, as you are! Herr Chamberlain thinking: "Impertinent Mozart. I must speak to the Emperor at once!" Herr Prefect thinking: "Ignorant Mozart. Debasing opera with his vulgarity!" Herr Court Composer thinking: "German Mozart. What can he finally know about music?" And Mozart himself, in the middle, thinking: "I'm just a good fellow. Why do they all disapprove of me?" [*Excitedly to* VAN SWIETEN] That's why opera is important, Baron. Because it's realer than any play! A dramatic poet would have to put all those thoughts down one after another to represent this second of time. The composer can put them all down at once—and still make us hear each one of them. Astonishing device—a vocal quartet! [*More and more excited*] I tell you I want to write a finale lasting half an hour! A quartet becoming a quintet becoming a sextet becoming a septet. On and on, wider and wider—all sounds multiplying and rising together— and then together making a sound entirely new. . . . I bet you that's how God hears the world! Millions of sounds ascending at once and mixing in His ear to become an *unending music,* unimaginable to us! [*To* SALIERI] That's our job! That's our *job,* we composers: to combine the inner minds of him and him and him, and her and her—the thoughts of chambermaids and Court Composers—and turn the audience into God.

> [*Pause.* SALIERI *stares at him, fascinated. Embarrassed,* MOZART *sounds a fart noise and giggles.*]

I'm sorry. I talk nonsense all day. It's incurable—ask Stanzerl. [*To* VAN SWIETEN] My tongue is stupid. My heart isn't.

VAN SWIETEN: No. You're a good fellow under all your nonsense: I know that. He'll make a fine new Brother, won't he, Salieri?

SALIERI: Better than I, Baron.

VAN SWIETEN: Just try, my friend, to be more serious with your gifts.

> [*He smiles, presses* MOZART's *hand and goes.* SALIERI *rises.*]

SALIERI: *Buona fortuna, Mozart.*

MOZART: *Grazie, Signore.* [*Rounding on* STRACK] Stop frowning, Herr Chamberlain. I'm a jackass. It's easy to be friends with a jackass: just shake his hoof.

> [*He forms his hand into a hoof. Warily* STRACK *takes it—then springs back as* MOZART *brays loudly like a donkey.*]

Hee-haw! . . . Tell the Emperor the opera's finished.

STRACK: Finished?

MOZART: Right here in my noddle. The rest's just scribbling. Goodbye.

STRACK: Good day to you.

MOZART: He's going to be proud of me. You'll see! [*He gives his flourish of the hand and goes out, delighted with himself.*]

STRACK: That young man *really is* . . .

SALIERI: [*Blandly*]. Very lively!

STRACK: [*Exploding*]. Intolerable! . . . *Intolerable!*
　　[STRACK *freezes in a posture of indignation.*]

SALIERI: [*To audience*]. How could I stop it? . . . How could I block this opera of *Figaro?* . . . Incredible to hear, within six weeks the Creature had finished the entire score!
　　[ROSENBERG *bustles in.*]

ROSENBERG: *Figaro* is complete! The first performance will be on May the first.

SALIERI: So soon?

ROSENBERG: There's no way we can stop it! [*A slight pause*]

SALIERI: [*Slyly*]. I have an idea. *Una piccola idea.*

ROSENBERG: What?

SALIERI: *Mi ha detto che c'è un balletto nel terzo atto?*

ROSENBERG: [*Puzzled*]. *Sì.*

STRACK: What does he say?

SALIERI: *E dimmi—non è vero che l'Imperatore ha proibito il balletto nelle sue opere?*

ROSENBERG: [*Realizing*]. *Uno balletto* . . . Ah!

SALIERI: *Precisamente.*

ROSENBERG: *Oh, capisco! Ma che meraviglia! Perfetto!* [*He laughs in delight.*] *Veramente ingegnoso!*

STRACK: [*Irritated*]. What is it? What is he suggesting?

SALIERI: See him at the theater.

ROSENBERG: Of course. Immediately. I'd forgotten. You are brilliant, Court Composer.

SALIERI: I? . . . I have said nothing. [*He moves away upstage.*]
　　[*The light begins to change, dimming down.*]

STRACK: [*Very cross*]. I must tell you that I resent this extremely. Mozart is right in some things. There is far too much Italian *chittero-chattero* at this court! Now please to inform me at once, what was just said?

ROSENBERG: [*Lightly*]. *Pazienza*, my dear Chamberlain. *Pazienza*. Just wait and see!

[*From upstage*, SALIERI *beckons to* STRACK. *Baffled and cross, the* CHAMBERLAIN *joins him. They watch together, unseen. The light dims further.*]

SCENE 5

An Unlit Theater

[*In the background, a projection of lamps glowing faintly in the darkened auditorium.* ROSENBERG *sits on one of the gold chairs, center.* MOZART *comes in quickly from the left, wearing another bright coat, and carrying the score of* Figaro. *He crosses to the fortepiano.*]

ROSENBERG: Mozart! . . . *Mozart!*

MOZART: Yes, Herr Director.

ROSENBERG: [*Agreeably*]. A word with you, please. Right away.

MOZART: Certainly. What is it?

ROSENBERG: I would like to see your score of *Figaro*.

MOZART: Oh, yes. Why?

ROSENBERG: Just bring it here to me. [*Unmoving*] Into my hand, please.

[MOZART *hands it to him, puzzled.* ROSENBERG *turns the pages.*]

Now tell me: did you not know that His Majesty has expressly forbidden ballet in his operas?

MOZART: Ballet?

ROSENBERG: Such as occurs in your third act.

MOZART: That is not a ballet, Herr Director. That is a dance at Figaro's wedding.

ROSENBERG: Exactly. A dance.

MOZART: [*Trying to control himself*]. But the Emperor doesn't mean to prohibit dancing when it's part of the story. He made that law to prevent insertions of stupid ballet like in French operas, and quite right too.

ROSENBERG: [*Raising his voice*]. It is not for you, Herr Mozart, to interpret the Emperor's edicts. Merely to obey them. [*He seizes the offending pages between his fingers.*]

MOZART: What are you doing? . . . What are you doing, Excellency?

ROSENBERG: Taking out what should never have been put in.

[*In a terrible silence,* ROSENBERG *tears out the pages.* MOZART *watches in disbelief. Upstage,* SALIERI *and* STRACK *look on together from the dimness.*]

Now, sir, perhaps in future you will obey imperial commands.

[*He tears out some more pages.*]

MOZART: But . . . But if all that goes—there'll be a hole right at the climax of the story . . . [*Crying out suddenly*] Salieri! This is Salieri's idea!

ROSENBERG: Don't be absurd.

SALIERI: [*To audience*]. How did he think of that?! Nothing I had ever done could possibly make him think of that on his own. Had God given him the idea?!

MOZART: It's a conspiracy. I can smell it. I can *smell* it! It's a conspiracy!

ROSENBERG: Control yourself!

MOZART: [*Howling*]. *But what do you expect me to do?* The first performance is two days off!

ROSENBERG: Write it over. That's your forte, is it not?—writing at speed.

MOZART: Not when the music's *perfect!* Not when it's absolutely perfect as it is! . . . [*Wildly*] I shall appeal to the Emperor! I'll go to him myself! I'll hold a rehearsal especially for him.

ROSENBERG: The Emperor does not attend rehearsals.

MOZART: He'll attend this one. Make no mistake—he'll come to this one! Then he'll deal with *you!*

ROSENBERG: This issue is simple. Write your act again today—or withdraw the opera. That's final.

[*Pause. He hands back the mutilated score to its composer.* MOZART *is shaking.*]

MOZART: You shit-pot.

[ROSENBERG *turns and walks imperturbably away from him.*] Sneaky—cliquey—

[*Serenely,* ROSENBERG *leaves the stage.*]

MOZART: [*Screeching after him*]. Count Orsini-Rosenberg! Rosen——! . . . Rosenclit! . . . I'll hold a rehearsal! You'll see! The Emperor will come! You'll see! You'll see! . . . *You'll see!!* [*He throws down his score in a storm of hysterical rage.*]

[*Upstage in the dimness,* STRACK *goes out, and* SALIERI *ventures down toward the shrieking little man.* MOZART *suddenly becomes aware of him. He turns, his hand shooting out in an involuntary gesture of accusation.*]

[*To* SALIERI] I am *forbidden!* . . . I am— But of course you know already.

SALIERI: [*Quietly*]. Know what?

[MOZART *flings away from him.*]

MOZART: [*Bitterly*]. No matter! [*He makes to go.*]

SALIERI: [*Always blandly*]. Mozart, permit me. If you wish, I will speak to the Emperor myself. Ask him to attend a rehearsal.

MOZART: [*Amazed*]. You wouldn't!

SALIERI: I cannot promise he will come, but I can try.

MOZART: [*Returning*]. Sir! . . .

SALIERI: Good day. [*He puts up his hands, barring further intimacy.*]

[MOZART *retreats to the fortepiano.*]

[*To audience*] Needless to say, I did nothing whatever in the matter. Yet—to my total stupefaction—

[STRACK *and* ROSENBERG *hurry on downstage.*]

—in the middle of the last rehearsal of *Figaro* next day . . .

[*The* EMPEROR JOSEPH *comes on from upstage.*]

JOSEPH: [*Cheerfully*]. Fêtes and fireworks! Fêtes and fireworks! Gentlemen, good afternoon!

SCENE 6

The Theater

SALIERI: [*To audience*]. Entirely against his usual practice, the Emperor *appeared!*

[STRACK *and* ROSENBERG *look at each other in consternation.* JOSEPH *seats himself excitedly on one of the gold chairs, facing out front. As with the premiere of* Seraglio *seen in Act One, he watches the audience as if it were the opera.*]

JOSEPH: I can't wait for this, Mozart, I assure you! *Je prévois des merveilles!*

MOZART: [*Bowing fervently*]. Majesty!

[*The courtiers sit also:* STRACK *on his right-hand side,* ROSENBERG *on his left.* SALIERI *also sits, near the keyboard.*]

SALIERI: [*To audience*]. What did this mean? Was this proof God had finally decided to defend Mozart against me? Was He engaging with me at last?

[MOZART *passes behind* SALIERI.]

MOZART: [*Earnestly, sotto voce*]. I am so grateful to you, I cannot express—

SALIERI: [*Aside, to him*]. Hush. Say nothing.

[MOZART *goes on quickly to the fortepiano and sits at it.*]

[*To audience*] One thing about the event seemed more than coincidence.

[*Music sounds faintly: the end of the third act of* Figaro, *just before the dance music starts.*]

Strangely, His Majesty had arrived at precisely the moment when the dancers would have begun, had not they and their music been entirely cut.

[*The music stops abruptly.*]

He and the rest of us watched the dramatic action proceed in total silence—whilst what should have been a party of celebrating peasants, dancing the fandango in the center of the stage, stood absolutely motionless, their arms frozen in the air.

[*Flanked by his* COURTIERS, *the* EMPEROR *stares out front, following with his eyes what is obviously a silent pantomime. His face expresses bewilderment.* ROSENBERG *watches his sovereign anxiously. Finally, the monarch speaks.*]

JOSEPH: I don't understand. . . . Is it modern?

MOZART: [*Jumping up nervously from the keyboard*]. No, Majesty.

JOSEPH: Then what?

MOZART: The Herr Director has removed a dance that would have occurred at this point.

JOSEPH: [*To* ROSENBERG]. Why was this done?

ROSENBERG: It's your own regulation, Sire. No ballet in your opera.

MOZART: [*Nervously*]. Majesty, this is not a ballet! . . . It is part of a wedding feast—entirely necessary for the story.

JOSEPH: Well, it certainly looks very odd the way it is. I can't say I like it.

MOZART: Nor do I, Majesty.

JOSEPH: Do you like it, Rosenberg?

ROSENBERG: It's not a question of liking, Majesty. Your own law decrees it.

JOSEPH: Yes. All the same, this is nonsense. Look at them: they're like waxworks up there.

ROSENBERG: Well, not exactly, Majesty.

JOSEPH: I don't like waxworks.

MOZART: Nor do I, Majesty.

JOSEPH: Well, who would? What do you say, Salieri?

SALIERI: Italians are fond of waxworks, Majesty. [*Pause*] Our religion is largely based upon them.

JOSEPH: You are *cattivo* again, Court Composer.

STRACK: [*Intervening creamily*]. Your Majesty, Count Rosenberg is very worried that if this music is put back, it will create the most unfortunate precedent. One will have thereafter to endure hours of dancing in opera.

JOSEPH: I think we can guard against that, you know, Chamberlain. I really think we can guard against hours of dancing. [*To* ROSENBERG] Please restore Herr Mozart's music.

ROSENBERG: But, Majesty, I must insist—

JOSEPH: [*With command*]. You will oblige me, Rosenberg! . . . I wish to hear Mozart's music. Do you understand me?

ROSENBERG: Yes, Majesty.

[MOZART *explodes with joy, jumps over a chair and throws himself at* JOSEPH's *feet*.]

MOZART: Oh, God, I thank Your Majesty! [*He kisses the* EMPEROR's *hand extravagantly, as at their first meeting.*] Oh, thank you—thank you—thank you, Sire, forever!

JOSEPH: [*Withdrawing hand*]. Yes, yes—very good. A little less enthusiasm, I beg you!

MOZART: [*Abashed*]. Excuse me.

[*The* EMPEROR *rises. All follow suit.*]

JOSEPH: Well—*there it is!*

SCENE 7

The First Performance of Figaro

[*The theater glows with light for the first performance of*
Figaro. COURTIERS *and* CITIZENS *come in swiftly.*
The EMPEROR *and his* COURT *resume their seats and the oth-*
ers quickly take theirs. In the front row we note KATHERINA
CAVALIERI, *all plumes and sequins, and* KAPELLMEISTER
BONNO—*older than ever. Behind them sit* CONSTANZE *and*
the VENTICELLI. *All of them stare out at the audience as if we*
were the opera they have come to see: people of fashion
down front; poorer people crowded into the Light Box,
upstage.

SALIERI *crosses as he speaks, to where two chairs have been*
placed side by side apart from the rest, on the left, to form his
box. On the chair upstage sits his good wife, TERESA—*more*
statuesque than ever.]

SALIERI: [*To audience*]. And so *Figaro* was produced in spite of all
my efforts. I sat in my box on May the first, 1786, and watched
it happen. A conspicuous defeat for me. And yet I was strangely
excited.

[*Faintly we hear Figaro singing the tune of "Non più*
andrai." The stage audience is obviously delighted: they
smile out front as they watch the (invisible) action.]

My march! My poor March of Welcome—now set to enchant
the world forever!

[*It fades. Applause. The* EMPEROR *rises, and with him the*
audience, to denote an intermission. JOSEPH *greets* KATHERINA
and BONNO. ROSENBERG *and* STRACK *go to* SALIERI's *box.*]

ROSENBERG: [*To* SALIERI]. Almost in your style, that last bit. But
more vulgar, of course. Far more obvious than you would
ever be.

STRACK: [*Drawling*]. Exactly!

[*A bell rings for the end of the intermission. The* EMPEROR *returns quickly to his seat. The audience sits. A pause. All look out front, unmoving.*]

SALIERI: [*Raptly and quietly, to audience*]. Trembling, I heard the second act. [*Pause*] The restored third act. [*Pause*] The astounding fourth. What shall I say to you who will one day hear this last act for yourselves? You will—because whatever else shall pass away, this must remain.

[*Faintly we hear the solemn closing ensemble from Act Four of* Figaro, *"Ah! Tutti contenti. Saremo così."*]

[*Over this*] The scene was night in a summer garden. Pinprick stars gleamed down on shaking summerhouses. Plotters glided behind pasteboard hedges. I saw a woman, dressed in her maid's clothes, hear her husband utter the first tender words he has offered her in years, only because he thinks she is someone else. Could one catch a realer moment? And how, except in a net of pure artifice? The disguises of opera had been invented for Mozart. [*He can barely look out at the "stage."*] The final reconciliation melted sight. [*Pause*] Through my tears I saw the Emperor . . . yawn.

[JOSEPH *yawns. The music fades. There is scant applause.* JOSEPH *rises and the* COURTIERS *follow suit.* MOZART *bows.*]

JOSEPH [*To* ROSENBERG]: [*Coolly*]. Most ingenious, Mozart. You are coming along nicely . . . I do think we must omit encores in future. It really makes things far too long. Make a note, Rosenberg.

ROSENBERG: Majesty.

[MOZART *lowers his head, crushed.*]

JOSEPH: Gentlemen, good night to you. Strack, attend me.

[JOSEPH *goes out, with* STRACK. *Director* ROSENBERG *gives* MOZART *one triumphant look and follows.* SALIERI *nods to his* WIFE, *who leaves with the audience. Only* CONSTANZE *lingers for a second, then she, too, goes. A pause.* MOZART *and* SALIERI *are left alone,* SALIERI *deeply shaken by the opera,* MOZART *deeply upset by its reception. He sits.*]

MOZART: [*Low*]. Herr Salieri.

SALIERI: Yes?

MOZART: What do you think? Do you think I am coming along nicely?

[*A pause*]

SALIERI: [*Moved*]. I think the piece is . . . extraordinary. I think it is . . . *marvelous*. Yes.

[*A pause*]

MOZART: I'll tell you what it is. It's the best opera yet written. That's what it is. And only I could have done it. No one else living!

[MOZART *walks away.* SALIERI *turns his head away swiftly, as if he has been slapped. They both freeze. The light changes. The* VENTICELLI *rush on.*]

V.1: Rosenberg is furious.

V.2: He'll never forgive Mozart.

V.1: He'll do anything to get back at him!

SALIERI: [*Rising, to audience*]. So it wasn't hard to get the piece canceled. I saw to it through the person of the resentful Director that in the entire year, *Figaro* was played only *nine times!* . . . My defeat finally turned into a victory. And God's response to my challenge remained as inscrutable as ever. . . . Was He taking any notice of me *at all?* . . .

[MOZART *breaks his freeze and comes downstage.*]

MOZART: *Withdrawn!* Absolutely no plans for its revival!

SALIERI: I commiserate with you, my friend. But if the public does not like one's work, one has to accept the fact gracefully. [*Aside, to audience*] And certainly they didn't.

V.1: [*Complaining*]. It's too complicated!

V.2: [*Complaining*]. Too tiresome!

V.1: All those morbid harmonies!

v.2: And never a good bang at the end of songs, so you know when to clap!

[*The* VENTICELLI *go off.*]

SALIERI: [*To audience*]. Obviously I would not need to plot too hard against his operas in future. I must concentrate on the man. I decided to see him as much as possible: to learn everything I could of his weaknesses.

SCENE 8

The Waldstädten Library

[SERVANTS *again bring on the wing chair.*]

MOZART: I'll go to England! England loves music. That's the answer!

SALIERI: [*To audience*]. We were *yet again* in the library of the Baroness Waldstädten—that room fated to be the scene of ghastly encounters between us! Again, too, the compensating *crema al mascarpone.*

[*He sits in the chair and eats greedily.*]

MOZART: I was there when I was a boy: they absolutely adored me. I had more kisses than you've had cakes! . . . When I was a child people loved me.

SALIERI: Perhaps they will again. Why don't you go to London and try?

MOZART: Because I have a wife and child and no money. I wrote to Papa to take the boy off my hands just for a few months so I could go—and he refused! . . . He's a bitter man, of course. After he'd finished showing me off around Europe he never went anywhere himself. He just stayed up in Salzburg year after

year, kissing the ring of the fartbishop and lecturing me! . . .
[*Confidentially*] The real thing is, you see, he's jealous. Under
everything he's jealous of *me!* He'll never forgive me for being
cleverer than he is.

[*He leans excitedly over* SALIERI's *chair like a naughty child.*]
I'll tell you a secret. Leopold Mozart is just a jealous, dried-up
old turd . . . And I actually detest him.

[*He giggles guiltily. The* VENTICELLI *appear quickly, and
address* SALIERI, *as* MOZART *freezes.*]

V.I: [*Solemnly*]. Leopold Mozart—

V.2: [*Solemnly*]. Leopold Mozart—

V.I & V.2: Leopold Mozart is dead!

[*They go off.* MOZART *recoils. A long pause.*]

SALIERI: Do not despair. Death is inevitable, my friend.

MOZART: [*Desperately*]. How will I go now?

SALIERI: What do you mean?

MOZART: In the world. There's no one else. No one who under-
stands the wickedness around. *I can't see it!* . . . He watched for
me all my life—and I betrayed him.

SALIERI: No!

MOZART: I talked against him.

SALIERI: *No!*

MOZART: [*Distressed*]. I married where he begged me not. I left
him alone. I danced and played billiards and fooled about—and
he sat by himself night after night in an empty house, and no
woman to care for him. . . . We used to sing a Kissing Song at
bedtime when I was small. His own silly words: [*Speaking
them*] "*Oragna figata fa! Marina gamina fa!*" Then Kiss—
Kiss—Kiss! . . . No one kissed him after I left, ever again.

[SALIERI *rises in concern.*]

SALIERI: Wolfgang. My dear Wolfgang! Don't accuse yourself. . . .
Lean upon me, if you care to. . . . Lean upon me.

[*He opens his arms in a wide gesture of benevolence.*
MOZART *approaches and is almost tempted to embrace. But*

at the last moment he avoids it and breaks away downstage
and falls on his knees, facing front.]

MOZART: [Crying out in anguish]. Papa!!

SALIERI: [To the audience]. So rose the Ghost Father in *Don Giovanni!*

SCENE 9

[*The two grim chords which open the overture to* Don Giovanni *sound loudly through the theater.* MOZART *seems to
quail under them, as he stares out front and sinks to his
knees. On the backdrop in the Light Box appears the silhouette of a giant black figure, in cloak and tricorne. It extends
its arms menacingly and engulfingly, toward its begetter.*]

SALIERI: A father more accusing than any in opera. So rose the figure of a Guilty Libertine, cast into Hell! . . . I looked on
astounded as from his ordinary life he made his art. We were
both ordinary men, he and I. Yet he from the ordinary created
legends—and I from legends created only the ordinary.

[*The figure fades. The music stops.* SALIERI *stands over the
kneeling* MOZART.]

Could I have not stopped my war? Shown him some pity? Oh
yes, my friends, at any time—if He above had shown me one
drop of it! Every day I set to work I prayed—I still prayed you
understand—"Make this one good in my ears! Just this one!
One!" But would He ever? . . . I heard my music calmed in con-
vention—not one breath of spirit to lift it off the shallows. And
I heard *his*—month after month—

[*We hear the exquisite strains of the terzetto "Soave il vento"
from* Così Fan Tutte. *Through the following, two girls in silhouette appear on the backcloth and walk away from us,
arm in arm, their backs to us, and disappear.*]

The spirit singing through it unstoppable, to my ears alone! I heard his comedy of the seduction of two sisters, *Così Fan Tutte: Thus do all women*. Aloysia and Constanze immortalized—two average girls turned into divinities: their sounds of surrender sweeter than the psalms of Heaven. [*To God in anguish*] "Grant this to me! . . . *Grant this to me!* . . . [*As "God"*] "No, no, no: I do not need you, Salieri! I have Mozart! Better for you to be silent!" *Ha Ha Ha Ha!*

[*The music cuts off.*]

The Creature's gleeful giggle was the laughter of God. I had to end it. How? DESTITUTION! Reduce the man to destitution. . . . Starve out the God!

[SERVANTS *enter and remove the wing chair.*]

SCENE 10

Vienna and the Palace of Schönbrunn

[MOZART *rises, a little frailer.*]

SALIERI: [*To* MOZART]. How do you fare today?

MOZART: Badly. I have no money, and no prospect of any.

SALIERI: It would not be too hard, surely.

[*Lights up on the Palace of Schönbrunn. The* EMPEROR *stands in the Light Box, in his golden space.*]

JOSEPH: We must find him a post.

SALIERI: [*To audience*]. One danger! The Emperor.

[SALIERI *goes upstage to* JOSEPH.] There's nothing available, Majesty.

JOSEPH: There's Chamber Composer, now that Gluck is dead.

SALIERI: [*Shocked*]. Mozart to follow Gluck?

JOSEPH: I won't have him say I drove him away. You know what a tongue he has.

SALIERI: Then grant him Gluck's post, Majesty, but not his salary. That would be wrong.

JOSEPH: Gluck got two thousand florins a year. What should Mozart get?

SALIERI: Four hundred. Light payment, yes, but for light duties.

JOSEPH: Perfectly fair. I'm obliged to you, Court Composer.

SALIERI: [*Bowing*]. Majesty. [*To audience*] And so easily done. Like many men obsessed with being thought generous, Joseph the Second was quintessentially stingy.

[MOZART *kneels to the* EMPEROR.]

JOSEPH: Herr Mozart, *vous nous faites honneur!*

[*Lights down on* JOSEPH, *but he stays where he is in the Light Box.* MOZART *and* SALIERI *come downstage.*]

MOZART: It's a damned insult. Not enough to keep a mouse in cheese for a week!

SALIERI: Regard it as a token, *caro Herr.*

MOZART: When I was young they gave me snuffboxes. Now it's tokens! And for what? Pom-pom for fireworks! Twang-twang for contredanzes!

SALIERI: I'm sorry it's made you angry. I'd not have suggested it if I'd known you'd be distressed.

MOZART: You suggested it?

SALIERI: I regret I was not able to do more.

MOZART: [*Overwhelmed*] Oh . . . *forgive me!* You're a good man! I see that now! You're a truly kind man—and I'm a monstrous fool!

[*He grasps* SALIERI'*s hand.*]

SALIERI: No, please . . .

MOZART: You make me ashamed. . . . You excellent man!

SALIERI: No, no, no, no—*s'il vous plaît.* A little less enthusiasm, I beg you!

[MOZART *laughs delightedly at this imitation of the Emperor.* SALIERI *joins in.*]

I shall see you soon again?

MOZART: Of course!

SALIERI: Why not visit me?

MOZART: [Warmly]. I will! . . . I promise!

SALIERI: *Bene.*

MOZART: *Bene.*

SALIERI: My friend. My new friend!

> [MOZART *giggles with pleasure and goes off.*]

> [*To audience*] Now, if ever, was the moment for God to crush me. I waited—and do you know what happened? I had just ruined Mozart's career at court. God rewarded me by granting me my dearest wish!

> [*The* VENTICELLI *come on.*]

V.1: Kapellmeister Bonno—

V.2: Kapellmeister Bonno—

V.1 & V.2: *Kapellmeister Bonno is dead!*

> [SALIERI *opens his mouth in surprise.*]

V.1: You are appointed—

V.2: By royal decree—

V.1: To fill his place!

> [*Lights full up on the* EMPEROR, *at the back. He is flanked by* STRACK *and* ROSENBERG, *standing like icons, as at their first appearance.*]

JOSEPH: [*Formally, as* SALIERI *turns and bows to him*]. First Royal and Imperial Kapellmeister to our court.

> [*The* VENTICELLI *applaud.*]

V.1: Bravo.

V.2: Bravo.

ROSENBERG: *Evviva,* Salieri!

STRACK: Well done, Salieri!

JOSEPH: [*Warmly*]. Dear Salieri. There it is!

> [*The lights go down on Schönbrunn. In the dark, the* EMPEROR *and his* COURT *leave the stage for the last time.* SALIERI *turns round, alarmed.*]

SALIERI: [*To audience*]. I was now truly alarmed. How long would I go unpunished?

V.I: Mozart looks appalling.

V.2: It must be galling, of course.

V.I: I hear he's dosing himself constantly with medicine.

SALIERI: For what?

V.2: Envy, I imagine.

V.I: Actually, I hear, syphilis.

SCENE II

The Prater

[*Fresh green trees appear on the backdrop. The light changes to yellow, turning the blue surround into a rich verdant green.*

MOZART *and* CONSTANZE *enter arm in arm. She is palpably pregnant and wears a poor coat and bonnet. His clothes are poorer, too, and his manner is hectic.* SALIERI *promenades with the* VENTICELLI.]

SALIERI: I met him next in the Prater.

MOZART: [*To* SALIERI]. Congratulations, sir!

SALIERI: I thank you. And to you both! [*To audience*] Clearly there was a change for the worse. His eyes gleamed, oddly, like a dog's when the light catches. [*To* MOZART] I hear you are not well, my friend.

[*He acknowledges* CONSTANZE, *who curtsies to him.*]

MOZART: It's nothing. A few pains. . . . And I do not sleep well, always.

SALIERI: Really?

MOZART: And I tend to have dreams now. Quite often.

CONSTANZE: [*Warningly*]. Wolferl!

SALIERI: Dreams? What kind? . . . You mean nightmares?

MOZART: Well . . .

CONSTANZE: Not now, dear.

SALIERI: No, please tell me.

MOZART: Actually, it's always the same one. A looming figure comes to me, wrapped in grey, doing this. [*Beckoning slowly*] It has no face. . . . What can it mean, do you think?

SALIERI: Surely you do not believe in dreams?

MOZART: No, of course not—really!

SALIERI: Surely *you* do not, madame?

CONSTANZE: I never dream, sir. Things are unpleasant enough to me, awake.

[SALIERI *bows*.]

MOZART: It's all fancy, of course!

CONSTANZE: [*Coldly*]. If Wolfgang had proper work, he might dream less, First Kapellmeister.

MOZART: [*Embarrassed, taking her arm*]. Stanzi, please! . . . Excuse us, sir. . . . Come, dearest. We are well enough, thank you.

[*Husband and wife continue their walk, and halt at the side of the stage. The light grows less sunny.* CONSTANZE *helps* WOLFGANG *off with his coat. He is revealed as wearing a Masonic apron.* CONSTANZE *leaves the stage.*]

V.1: He's growing freakish.

V.2: No question.

V.1: Grey figures with no faces!

SALIERI: [*Looking after him*]. His circumstances make him anxious, I fancy.

V.1: They've moved house again.

V.2: To the Rauhensteingasse. Number 970.

V.1: They must be desperate.

V.2: It's a real slum.

SALIERI: Does he earn money at all, apart from his post?

v.1: Nothing whatever.

v.2: I hear he's starting to beg.

v.1: They say he's written letters to twenty brother Masons.

SALIERI: Really?

v.2: And they're giving him money.

SALIERI: [*To audience*]. Of course! They *would!* . . . I had *forgotten* the Masons! *Naturally* they would relieve him—how *stupid* of me! . . . There could be no finally starving him with the Masons there to help! As long as he asked they would keep supplying his wants! . . . How could I stop it? And quickly! . . .

v.1: Lord Fugue is most displeased with him!

SALIERI: *Is* he?

SCENE 12

A Masonic Lodge

[*A huge golden emblem descends, encrusted with Masonic symbols.*

Enter VAN SWIETEN. *He, too, is wearing the ritual apron over his sober clothes. The two men clasp hands in fraternal greeting.*

VAN SWIETEN: [*Gravely*]. This is not good, Brother. The lodge was not created for you to beg from.

MOZART: What else can I do?

VAN SWIETEN: Give concerts, as you used to do.

MOZART: I have no subscribers left, Baron. I am no longer fashionable.

VAN SWIETEN: I am not surprised! You write tasteless comedies which give offense. I warned you, often enough.

MOZART: [*Humbly*]. You did. I admit it.

VAN SWIETEN: I will send you some fugues of Bach tomorrow. You can arrange those for my Sunday concert. You shall have a small fee.

MOZART: Thank you, Baron.

[VAN SWIETEN *nods and goes out.* SALIERI *steps forward. He, too, wears the Masonic apron.*]

[*Shouting after* VAN SWIETEN] I cannot live by arranging Bach!

SALIERI: [*Sarcastically*]. A generous fellow.

MOZART: All the same, I'll have to do it. If he were to turn the lodge against me, I'd be finished. My brother Masons virtually keep me now.

SALIERI: Wolfgang, it's embarrassing, I know—but you must allow me to relieve you also.

MOZART: No!

SALIERI: If it is the duty of a Mason to help—how much more of a friend.

MOZART: Not another word! I would never take money from you. That friendship is worth all the gold in the world. Please—no more of that!

SALIERI: You overwhelm me.

MOZART: I'll manage: you'll see! Things are looking up already. I've had a marvelous proposal from Schikaneder. He's a new member of this lodge.

SALIERI: Schikaneder? The actor?

MOZART: Yes. He owns a theater in the suburbs.

SALIERI: Well, more of a music hall, surely?

MOZART: Yes. . . . He wants me to write him a vaudeville—something for ordinary German people. Isn't that a wonderful idea? . . . He's offered me half the receipts when we open.

SALIERI: Nothing in advance?

MOZART: He said he couldn't afford anything. I know it's not much of an offer. But a popular piece about brotherly love could celebrate everything we believe as Masons!

SALIERI: It certainly could! . . . Why don't you put the Masons *into* it?

MOZART: Into an opera? . . . I couldn't.

[SALIERI *laughs, to indicate that he was simply making a joke.*]

All the same—what an idea!

SALIERI: [*Earnestly*]. Our rituals are secret, Wolfgang.

MOZART: I needn't copy them exactly. I could adapt them a little.

SALIERI: Well. . . . It would certainly be in a great cause.

MOZART: Brotherly love!

SALIERI: Brotherly love!

[*They both turn and look solemnly at the great golden emblem hanging at the back.*]

SALIERI: [*Warmly*]. Take courage, Wolfgang. It's a glorious idea.

MOZART: It is, isn't it? It really is!

SALIERI: Of course say nothing until it is done.

MOZART: Not a word.

SALIERI: [*Making a sign: closed fist*]. Secret!

MOZART: [*Making a similar sign*]. Secret!

SALIERI: Good.

[*He steps out of the scene downstage.*]

[*To audience*] And if that didn't finish him off with the Masons—nothing would!

[*The gold emblem withdraws. We hear the merry dance of Monostatos and the hypnotized slaves from* The Magic Flute: *"Das Klinget so heimlich, Das Klinget so schön!"* MOZART *stands entranced downstage, hearing it too—then moves smilingly into his apartment, right, to write it down. Simultaneously, to the tinkling of the glockenspiel,* SERVANTS *bring in a long plain table loaded with manuscripts, bottles and a plain stool, which they place beside it.* MOZART *sits to work, as* CONSTANZE *appears wearily from the back, enters this dingy room and sits too.*]

At the same time, upstage left, two other SERVANTS *have placed the little gilded table bearing a loaded cake-stand and three of the gilded chairs from* SALIERI's *resplendent salon. We now have in view two contrasting apartments.*

As soon as the Masonic emblem withdraws, the music fades down and the VENTICELLI *appear to* SALIERI.]

SCENE 13

Mozart's Apartment; Salieri's Apartment

v.1: *Mozart* is delighted with himself!

v.2: He's writing a secret opera!

v.1: [*Crossly*]. And won't tell anyone its theme.

v.2: It's really too tiresome.

[*The* VENTICELLI *go off. The music stops.*]

SALIERI: He told *me*. He told me everything! . . . Initiation ceremonies. Ceremonies with blindfolds. All rituals copied from the Masons! . . . He sat at home preparing his own destruction. A home where life grew daily more grim.

[*He goes upstage and sits on one of his gilded chairs, devouring a cake.* MOZART *also sits at his table, wrapped in a blanket, and writing the music. Opposite him* CONSTANZE *sits on a stool, wrapped in a shawl.*]

CONSTANZE: I'm cold . . . I'm cold all day . . . Hardly surprising since we have no firewood.

MOZART: Papa was right. We end exactly as he said. Beggars.

CONSTANZE: It's all his fault.

MOZART: Papa's?

CONSTANZE: He kept you a baby all your life.

MOZART: I don't understand. . . . You always loved Papa.

CONSTANZE: *I* did?

MOZART: You adored him. You told me so often.

[*Slight pause*]

CONSTANZE: [*Flatly*]. I hated him.

MOZART: What?

CONSTANZE: And he hated *me*.

MOZART: That's absurd. He loved us both very much. You're being extremely silly now.

CONSTANZE: Am I?

MOZART: [*Airily*]. Yes you are: little-wife-of-my-heart!

CONSTANZE: Do you want to know what I really thought of your father? . . . Do you remember the fire we had last night, because it was so cold you couldn't even get the ink wet? You said "What a blaze," remember? "What a blaze!" All those old papers going up? Well, my dear, those old papers were just all your father's letters, that's all—every one he wrote since the day we married.

MOZART: *What?*

CONSTANZE: Every one! All the letters about what a ninny I am— what a bad housekeeper I am! Every one!

MOZART: Stanzi!

CONSTANZE: Shit on him! . . . *Shit on him!*

MOZART: *You bitch!*

CONSTANZE: [*Savagely*]. At least it kept us warm! What else will do that? Perhaps we should dance! You love to dance, Wolferl— let's dance! Dance to keep warm! [*Grandly*] Write me a contredanze, Mozart! It's your job to write dances, isn't it?

[*Hysterical, she snatches up his manuscripts from the table and scatters them over the floor—pulling up her skirts and dancing roughly round the room like a demented peasant, to the tune of "Non più andrai"!*]

CONSTANZE: [*Singing savagely*]. *Non più andrai, farfallone amoroso—notte e giorno d'intorno girando!*

MOZART: [*Shrieking*]. Stop it! Stop it!

[*He rises and tries to seize her.*] Stanzi-marını! Marını-bini!

Don't *please!* . . . Please—please I beg you! . . . Look. There's a kiss! Where's it coming from? Right out of that corner! There's another one—all wet, all sloppy wet, coming straight to you! Kiss—kiss—kiss—kiss!

[*She pushes him roughly away.*]

CONSTANZE: Get off!

[*A long pause*]

MOZART: I'm frightened, Stanzi. . . . Something awful's happening to me. The pains stay. And the dream! . . .

CONSTANZE: [*Quietly*]. I can't bear it. I can't bear much more of this.

MOZART: [*Absorbed in himself*]. The Figure's like this now— [*Beckoning more urgently*]—Here. Come here. Here . . . Its face still hidden. Always hidden.

CONSTANZE: [*Crying out*]. Stop it, for God's sake! Stop it! . . . Stop! . . . It's me who's frightened. . . . *Me!* . . . You frighten me. . . . If you go on like this I'll leave you. I swear it.

MOZART: [*Shocked*]. Stanzi!

CONSTANZE: I mean it . . . I do. . . .

[*She puts her hand to her stomach, as if in pain.*]

MOZART: I'm sorry. . . . Oh God, I'm sorry . . . I'm sorry, I'm sorry, I'm sorry, I'm sorry! . . . Come here to me, little-wife-of-my-heart! Come . . . Come . . .

[*He kneels and coaxes her to him. She comes half-reluctantly, half-willingly.*]

Who am I? . . . Quick: tell me. Hold me and tell who I am. Who?—come on.

CONSTANZE: Pussy-wussy.

MOZART: Who else?

CONSTANZE: Miaowy-powy.

MOZART: And you're squeaky-peeky. And Stanzi-manzi. And Bini-gini!

[*She surrenders.*]

CONSTANZE: Wolfi-polfi!

MOZART: Poopy-peepee!

[*They giggle.*]

CONSTANZE: Now don't be stupid.

MOZART: [*Insistent: like a child*]. Come on—do it. Do it. . . . Let's do it. . . . "Poppy."

[*They play a private game, gradually doing it faster, on their knees.*]

CONSTANZE: Poppy.

MOZART: [*Changing it*]. Pappy.

CONSTANZE: [*Copying*]. Pappy.

MOZART: Pappa.

CONSTANZE: Pappa.

MOZART: Pappa-pappa!

CONSTANZE: Pappa-pappa!

MOZART: Pappa-pappa-pappa-pappa!

CONSTANZE: Pappa-pappa-pappa-pappa!

[*They rub noses.*]

TOGETHER: Pappa-pappa-pappa-pappa! Pappa-pappa-pappa-pappa!

CONSTANZE: *Ah!*

[*She suddenly cries out in distress, and clutches her stomach.*]

MOZART: Stanzi! . . . Stanzi, what is it?

[*The* VENTICELLI *hurry in.*]

SALIERI: And suddenly she was delivered! A boy!

V.2: Poor little imp.

V.1: To be born to that couple.

V.2: In that room.

V.1: With that money.

V.2: And the Father a baby himself.

[*During the above,* CONSTANZE *has slowly risen, and divested herself of her stuffed apron—thereby ceasing to be pregnant. Now she turns sorrowfully and walks briskly upstage and off it.* MOZART *follows her for a few steps, alarmed. He halts.*]

V.1: And now I hear—

V.2: Now I hear—

v.1: Something more has happened.

v.2: Even stranger.

> [MOZART *picks up a bottle, then moves swiftly into* SALIERI's *salon. He looks distracted.*]

MOZART: *She's gone!*

SALIERI: What do you mean?

> [*The* VENTICELLI *slip away.*]

MOZART: Constanze's gone away. Just for a while, she says. She's taken the baby and gone to Baden. To the spa. It'll cost us the last money we had.

SALIERI: But *why?*

MOZART: [*Distressed*]. She's right to go! It's my fault! She thinks I'm mad.

SALIERI: Surely not?

MOZART: Perhaps I am. I think maybe I am. . . .

SALIERI: Wolfgang—

MOZART: [*Terrified*]. This morning I saw a figure much like the one in my dream—only *clear*, not misty. And this time I was *awake!*—in my room—*in broad daylight!* . . . Oh God, it *spoke!* It said—it was terrible! . . .

SALIERI: Wolfgang, calm yourself. Just tell me what happened.

> [*Pause.* MOZART *struggles to control himself.*]

MOZART: I was seated at my table working. Suddenly there came three sharp knocks at the door, and a Figure entered, all muffled in grey. But now it had a *face! A death's-head!*—glaring at me with frozen eyes sunk deep in little caves of bone! . . . And then it *spoke!* A horrible sound like a man hissing. . . . It said, "Wolfgang Mozart: you are required now by my Master to write a Requiem Mass. . . . It must be finished completely when you see me next. And you will tell no one." I asked, "Who has died? Who is this Requiem for? . . . And who is your Master?" . . . [*Again hissing*] "Know only this: He will be much displeased with you if it is not ready when required! Therefore write quickly!" Then he turned and left. I went to the window to see him reappear down in the street, but he didn't. He had vanished!

[*Pause.* SALIERI *goes to him.*]

SALIERI: This is simply morbid fancy, my friend. [*Earnestly touching* MOZART'*s head*] It was all in there—and only there.

MOZART: I'm being silly, aren't I?

SALIERI: [*Smiling*]. Yes, I think you are.

MOZART: Yet it had the force of real things! . . . [*In relief*] No wonder Stanzi left. I frightened her away. Poor girl. . . . And now she'll miss the Vaudeville—and I wrote so much of it for her—to make her laugh.

SALIERI: [*Surprised*]. You mean it's finished? So soon? It's only been a month.

MOZART: Oh music is easy: it's marriage that's hard.

SALIERI: I long to see it.

MOZART: The theater isn't grand. It's just a popular music hall. No one from court will be there.

SALIERI: Do you think that matters to me? I would travel anywhere for a work by you!

MOZART: Saturday will be the first performance.

SALIERI: Good! [*Sly*] I know I'm no substitute for your little wife, but I know someone who will chase away your glooms.

MOZART: [*Laughing like a child*]. Saturday night then!

SALIERI: Saturday!

[MOZART *grabs* SALIERI'*s hand gleefully, then turns out of the scene.*]

[*Light change.*]

[*To the audience*]. What was happening? Could that grim Figure actually exist? A skull-faced ghost ordering a Mass from beyond the grave? Clearly not!

MOZART [*Turning back*]: [*Light change*]. Are you ready? It's time for the performance!

SALIERI: I can't wait! A Vaudeville by you—*che diletto assoluto!* ...
   And—if you recall, I promised to cheer you up. Well—behold!
   [KATHERINA CAVALIERI *enters, now fatter, and wearing an
   elaborate plumed hat.*]
MOZART: [*Bowing delightedly*]. Katherina!
   [*She curtsies to* MOZART *and takes his arm.*]
SALIERI: [*To the audience*]. And so to the opera we went—a
   strange band of three! [*The other two freeze.*] The First
   Kapellmeister—sleek as a cat. His mistress—now fat and feath-
   ered like the great songbird she'd become. And Mozart—odd-
   looking and drunk on the cheap wine which was now his
   constant habit. [*They unfreeze.*] We went into the suburbs—to a
   crowded music hall—in a tenement!

SCENE 14

The Theater by the Weiden

[*Sudden noise. Benches are brought in and placed horizontally across the stage. A crowd of working-class Germans
swarms in from the back: a chattering mass of humanity
though which the three have to push their way to the front.
The long table is also pushed horizontally, and the rowdy
audience piles on top of it, smoking pipes and chewing
sausages. Unobserved.* BARON VAN SWIETEN *comes in also,
and stands at the back.*]
MOZART: You must be indulgent now! It's my first piece of this
   kind!
   [*The three sit on the front bench:* MOZART *sick and emaci-
   ated;* CAVALIERI *blowsy and bedizened;* SALIERI *as elegant as
   ever.*]

SALIERI: We sat as he wished us to, among ordinary Germans. The smell of sweat and sausage was almost annihilating!

[CAVALIERI *presses a* mouchoir *to her sensitive nose.*]

[*To* MOZART] This is so exciting!

MOZART: [*Happily*]. Do you think so?

SALIERI: [*Looking about him*]. Oh yes! This is exactly the audience we should be writing for! Not the dreary court . . . As always—you show the way.

[*The audience freezes.*]

[*To audience*] As always, he did. My pungent neighbors rolled on their benches at the jokes—

[*They unfreeze, briefly, to demonstrate this mirth.*]

And I, in their midst, heard *The Magic Flute.*

[*They freeze again as the serene tenor song with flute "Wie stark ist nicht dein Zauberton!" is heard, and the audience becomes immediately enraptured from its orchestral intro-duction onward.*]

He had put the Masons into it right enough. Oh yes—but how? He had turned them into a secret order of Priests. I heard voices calling out of ancient temples. I saw a vast sun rise on a time-less land where animals danced and children floated, and by its rays all the poisons we feed each other drawn up and burnt away!

[*A giant sun does indeed rise inside the Light Box, and stand-ing in it the gigantic silhouette of a priestly figure robed in Egyptian costume and headdress, extending its arms in uni-versal greeting.*]

SALIERI: And in this sun—behold—I saw his father. No more an accusing figure but *forgiving*—the highest Priest of the Order—his hands extended to the world in love! Mozart feared Leopold no longer. A final Legend had been made. . . . And oh, the sound of that newfound peace in him—so tender—so *serene!* . . . *There* was *The Magic Flute*—there beside me!

[*He points to* MOZART, *who jumps up on the bench excitedly*

*to great applause and acknowledges the clapping with his
arms flung wide, a bottle in his hand. He turns back to us—
his eyes staring. All freeze.*]

How could this be?—in the face of everything I had done to
him. . . . Was this his response to all my injuries—these priceless
sighs of exaltation?

[*The music stops. In slow motion* MOZART *turns to* SALIERI—
and SALIERI, *moved, reaches up a hand to him also in slow
motion.*]

[*Moved*] Wolfgang!—

[*Still slowly,* MOZART *reaches down to him, but just as their
hands touch, they are interrupted by a furious* BARON VAN
SWIETEN.]

VAN SWIETEN: [*Calling out*]. Mozart!

[*Outraged, he pushes his way to the front through the crowd
of dispersing* CITIZENS.]

MOZART: [*Turning joyfully to greet him*]. Baron! *You* here!—How
wonderful of you to come!

SALIERI: [*To audience*]. I had, of course, suggested it.

VAN SWIETEN: [*With cold fury*]. What have you done?

MOZART: Excellency?

VAN SWIETEN: You have put our rituals into a vulgar show!

MOZART: No, sir.

VAN SWIETEN: They are plain for all to see! And to laugh at! . . .
You have betrayed the Order.

MOZART: [*In horror*]. No!

SALIERI: Baron, a word with you—

VAN SWIETEN: Don't speak for him, Salieri! [*To* MOZART, *with
frozen contempt*] You were ever a crude vulgarian we hoped to
mend. Stupid, hopeless task! Now you are a betrayer as well. I
shall never forgive you! And depend on it, I shall ensure that no
Freemason or person of distinction will do so in Vienna so long
as I have life!

SALIERI: Baron, please, I must speak!

VAN SWIETEN: No, sir! Leave alone. [*To* MOZART] I did not look for this reward, Mozart. Never speak to me.

[*He goes out.* CAVALIERI, *embarrassed, goes out another way. The lights change. The benches are taken off.* SALIERI *watches* MOZART, *who stands stunned.*]

SCENE 15

Salieri's Apartment, and Outside in Vienna

SALIERI: Wolfgang? . . .

[MOZART *shakes his head sharply—and walks away from him, upstage, desolate and stunned.*]

Wolfgang—all is not lost.

[MOZART *enters his apartment, and freezes.*]

[*To audience*] But of course it was! Now he was ruined. Broken and shunned by all men of influence. He did not even get his half receipts from the opera.

[*He sits. The* VENTICELLI *come in.*]

V.1: Schikaneder pays him nothing.

V.2: Schikaneder cheats him.

V.1: Gives him enough for liquor.

V.2: And keeps all the rest.

SALIERI: [*Ironically*]. I couldn't have managed it better myself.

[MOZART *sits despairingly at his table, in the gloom. He takes up a wine bottle—but it is empty. Suddenly he starts to write, with great vigor, dropping finished pages on the floor. Through this the* VENTICELLI *speak.*]

V.1: And as for Mozart—

v.2: The poor fellow—

SALIERI: [*Urgently*]. What about him? . . . I've heard nothing from him in days . . . What is he doing?

V.1 & V.2: [*Together*]. We don't know!

V.1: [*Confidentially*]. He's become really odd, sir.

V.2: Turned dreadfully strange!

V.1: Stays in his apartment all day.

V.2: Burns his candle all night.

> [MOZART *jumps up quickly, and faces front, downstage, looking out in alarm.*]

V.1: But appears over and over at his window—

V.2: Staring wildly down into the street.

V.1: Twitching!

V.2: Trembling!

V.1: Like a man deeply disordered!

V.2: Or one driven out of his mind!

> [SALIERI *looks at them startled.* MOZART *sits again, and resumes his feverish writing.*]

V.1: [*Hushed*]. In fact, the rumor is—

V.2: [*Hushed*]. The rumor is, sir—

> [*Pause*]

SALIERI: What? . . . *Say it!*

V.1 & V.2: *Our Wolfgang has lost his wits!*

> [*Pause.* SALIERI *makes a sharp gesture of dismissal. The* VENTICELLI *leave quickly. Light change.*]

SALIERI: [*To audience, very disturbed*]. Was it true? Could it be possible?—*Madness?* . . . I'd never thought of that!—him retreating into that terrible refuge. Yet there would lie my Victory. Loss of wits must surely mean loss of talent! . . . Triumph surged up through me. He was disarmed at last! . . . And at that same moment came chill—deep-spreading chill. [*Pause*] Was this what I had actually done? Driven a man mad? . . . [*Urgently*] I had to know. See for myself. Spy on him unseen— immediately! . . . I couldn't keep away!

[*Two o'clock strikes. The* VALET *enters swiftly and wraps his master in a long, loose cloak of grey, hands him a wide grey hat and leaves.* SALIERI *speaks through this, finally pulling the hat low on his brow, and moving downstage.*]

And so it was, incredibly late one freezing night in November 1791, I found myself hurrying secretly across the empty city, under a churning sky and a hidden moon, seeking his lodgings where I had never been—no notion what I might see!

[*He stops, facing the audience.*]

There was my goal: that dingy alley, the Rauhensteingasse.

[*He looks up.*]

Only one window alight, above me. . . . Stealthily I stationed myself to watch it from the shadows below—but instantly, as if sensing me, he *appeared!*

[MOZART *rises and also comes downstage to face the audience. He seems now to be seriously ill.*]

A drawn face distorted by fear, staring straight down at my motionless figure, standing deep-cloaked against the cold. A cry came faintly from behind the dirty glass, and through it his mouth began shaping frenzied words: "*More!* . . . *More!* . . . *More time!* . . . *Time!* [*Desperately*] "*Oh pleeeeease!*"

[*Both men now stand staring at the audience:* MOZART *mimes speaking his words as* SALIERI *sounds them aloud.*]

I stood frozen in alarm—until suddenly, without warning, the *moon sprang full out* from behind a cloud, and spilled its merciless light all down me! He saw clearly who it was. And there was nothing for it but to *greet* him—cheerfully! . . .

[SALIERI *takes off his hat and gives a ghastly smile, and a bow.* MOZART *mimes, as before.*]

With a gesture of pure *relief,* he flung open the casement and called down.

MOZART: *Signore!* . . . Oh how wonderful! . . . Come up! . . . *Come up!!* [*Inventing joyfully*] Come up, come up and join the fun! There's nothing to eat, not even a bun! And alas and alack, there's nothing to drink. But bottles and bottles and bottles of ink! . . . [*He giggles delightedly.*] Ascend, if you please!

SALIERI: [*To audience*]. Will-less, I climbed his stairs with stone feet.

[*Faintly the rising and falling scale passage from the Overture sounds in repetition, and to this hollow music* SALIERI *moves slowly upstage.* MOZART *moves also. They face each other. The music fades.*]

He was waiting at the top.

MOZART: A thousand welcomes, sir. Enter, if you please, the Palazzo Amadeo!

[*He gives a courtly flourish, indicating his room.* SALIERI *"enters" it, looking around him.*]

SCENE 16

Mozart's Apartment

SALIERI: Now for the first time I saw the place to which I had consigned him. A filthy chamber in total disorder. Empty bottles everywhere—discarded linen—and across the floor an inky pavement of fresh manuscripts, stirring in icy gusts from ill-fitting windows. . . . I knew *at once* what these must be! . . . As for his face, it held a look I'd never seen before—not madness at all, but some deep-possessing physical *sickness!*

MOZART: Tell me, my friend—what are you doing here so late? It *is* late, isn't it?

SALIERI: I came to see you. I've been concerned. . . . Let me ask what *you* are doing. Surely not working at this hour?

MOZART: [*Guiltily*]. No, not really!

SALIERI: [*Indicating the floor*]. Well, what's all this?

MOZART: Nothing! Just silliness. . . . A new piece.

SALIERI: [*Sharply*]. The Requiem! *It's the Requiem*—isn't it?

MOZART: [*Defensively*]. I know. It's stupid. That Messenger isn't real—you told me and I believe you. All the same, there's no point in taking chances, is there? If he suddenly appeared and there was nothing for him, I'd look foolish. Mind you, it's not nearly finished. Time was when I could have finished a Mass in a week. Not anymore. . . . To be exact, I'm feeling very poorly.

SALIERI: [*Concerned*]. My friend!

MOZART: It's true. My body hurts all day—my joints, my head. . . . And I know why! [*Confidentially*] I've been poisoned.

SALIERI: Poisoned?

MOZART: They say the Masons poison people who offend them! [*In panic*]. I didn't mean that! . . . [*Defiant*]. I'll tell you one thing, though. If he comes too soon, that Messenger, I'll say it to his face: "Tell your Master from me, if He takes me too quick, there won't *be* a Mass—so there!" He can hiss at me all he likes.

[*Pause*]

SALIERI: [*Carefully*]. My friend, what are you saying?

MOZART: Isn't it obvious? [*Pause*] It's for me, that's all.

SALIERI: What is?

MOZART: [*Factually*]. The Mass. It's for me. Myself. . . . It's ordered. I am to write my own!

[*Pause*]

There's no need ordering a Requiem if no one's going to die! . . . You know, the worst thing is denying me proper time. That shames me. I've never done that in my life—offered unfinished work.

[SALIERI *looks at him astounded.*]

I wonder, sir, if you could oblige me—take a look at it, just a page or two, and tell me if it's worthy. You see, I don't know anymore. Everything's leaving me. Now the *sounds*: they're running away! My hand is tired—it's written too much—it can't catch the notes now. . . . The Kyrie's finished—you only need read that.

[*He picks a few pages of manuscript off the table.*]

Kyrie the first theme—Eleison the second: both together make a double fugue. My father would've approved that at least. He'd say, "Only you, my boy. Only you could have done it!". . . *Please.*

[*Urgently he proffers the pages. Reluctantly* SALIERI *takes them and sits to read. Immediately we hear the somber opening of the Requiem Mass. Over this* MOZART *speaks.*]

Oh, it began so well, my life. Once the world was so full, so happy. All the journeys—all the carriages—all the rooms of smiles! Everyone smiled at me once—the King at Schönbrunn: the Princess at Versailles—they lit my way *personally* to the keyboard! Papa bowing, bowing, bowing with such joy! . . . "Chevalier Mozart, my miraculous son!" . . . Why has it all gone? . . . Was I so wicked? . . . [*Outraged*] *Why must I go?*

[SALIERI *is reading the score with increasing disturbance. Suddenly he crumples the paper. Instantly the sound stops. He sits, deeply shaken and alarmed.*]

[*Watching him, in panic*]. It's bad, isn't it? It's *bad!*

SALIERI: [*Slowly*]. Bad? . . . It will help the ages to mourn.

MOZART: [*Fervently*]. *Oh grazie. . . . Grazie, Signore!*

[*He reaches out in gratitude, and freezes.*]

SALIERI: [*To audience*]. What could I say? In my shaking hands I held a terrible contradiction that only Art can show. Something *immortal*—yet stinking of *death. Indestructible*—and yet *rotting!* [*He gives a faint gasp.*] Suddenly I was seized by an overwhelming horror!

MOZART: [*Unfreezing*]. I bless you.

SALIERI: [*Still to audience, clutching the manuscript*]. Who was this *for*, this appalling music? Not himself. Of course not himself! What need to mourn a man who will live *forever?*

MOZART: I bless you, *Signore!*

SALIERI: [*Still to audience*]. *Who*, then?

[*He rises in growing distress.*]

MOZART: I cannot believe you came here. Sought me out. No one seeks me anymore. . . . Only you—my one Protector—[*Kneeling and laying his cheek against the man's hand*]—Antonio.

[*In this gesture he freezes again. The grim Kyrie is now heard once more. Over it in huge anguish* SALIERI *speaks.*]

SALIERI: [*To audience*]. I stood there—his despairing Mass sounding over and over in my head its gigantic lamentation—and knew *absolutely* who it was for! . . . *The boy!* . . . That eager boy who once stumbled around the fields of Lombardy, singing up his anthems to his Lord. [*Pause*] In ten years of unrelenting spite—I had destroyed *myself!*

[*The music stops.* SALIERI *touches* MOZART's *head.*]

And then—any feelings still left uncorrupted in me rose up, crying, "*End this!* Before it is too late! . . . *Confess! Confess to him!* . . . Get from *him* whatever absolution he can possibly grant. He—he alone!—the Creature you have broken. . . . How else can you live on after?"

[*A pause,* SALIERI *tries to find the strength to begin.*]

Wolfgang, you must hear me.

[MOZART *raises his head and looks at him.*]

You are right. You are poisoned. It is true.

MOZART: What do you mean?—

SALIERI: By me! No one else. . . . We are both poisoned. *Both—together.*

MOZART: [*Bewildered*]. I don't understand.

SALIERI: Both. Both. With each other.

[*Nervously* MOZART *rises.*]

MOZART: Excuse me, sir. I'm stupid sometimes. . . .

[*He starts to back away.* SALIERI *follows him. The scene quickens.*]

SALIERI: You with me. I with you! [*In his urgency he relapses into*

his native tongue, gesturing urgently.] Si!—Tutti e due! Tutti e
due! . . . Noi siamo avvelenati! . . . Tu con me!—Io con te!
[*He holds up the manuscript Kyrie.*]
I eat what God gives me. Dose after dose. For all of life!
[*Savagely he tears off with his teeth a piece of the manuscript
and chews it fiercely—then spits it out.*]
AVVELENATI!
[*He throws out his arms.*]
Eccomi! Antonio Salieri! . . . Il tuo Nemico! . . . Il tuo Assas-
sino! [*In sudden pity*] Il tua morte!
[*He clasps his breast in a sign for swearing, but* MOZART *only
bursts out laughing and clapping delightedly.*]
MOZART: *Bravo! Bravissimo!* . . . *Signore,* are you perhaps a little
tiddly? [*Amused*] I think you *are!* . . . Tiddly-widdly! [*Mock
scolding*] You had some before you came! I thought that might
be so!
SALIERI: [*Desperate*]. Wolfgang, you must hear me now.
MOZART: [*Giggling defensively*]. Tiddly-widdly-piddly! . . . Well,
why not? It's a cold night. . . . And a good performance!
SALIERI: [*Raising his voice*]. No—you have to listen! . . . Under-
stand what has been done to you.
MOZART: What?? . . . Why are you being like this? . . . It's stupid!
[*With sudden apprehension*] Why have you come here? . . .
What do you want? . . .
[*He retreats across the room to the table.* SALIERI *moves after
him relentlessly. His manner becomes increasingly out of
control.*]
SALIERI: Don't you know at all what I have endured from you? . . .
From the day you appeared I have lived in Hell. . . . What I did
to you was nothing to what you did to *me!*
MOZART: Stop this, please, *Signore.* I don't know what you're saying!
SALIERI: My God smiled—and *permitted* it! . . . Whatever I did—
you would fill the world! [*Outraged*] You left me with *nothing!*
[*He forces himself to smile, his manner wheedling.*]

No matter. You're not to blame. It's His will. I don't hate *you*—you're only an instrument.

MOZART: *Signore*, please! . . . This makes no sense.

SALIERI: [*Agreeing, gleefully*]. No! No!—None! . . . And now you're going. You're right: He's finished with you. You're too feeble to be used anymore. Worn through! . . . He can only use. And He does not care Amadeus. God does not care, Amadeus. He cares nothing for whom He uses—nothing for whom He denies! We are equal at least in *that*. . . . Ha?

MOZART: [*Distressed*]. Stop this! Stop it at once! You're frightening!

[*Like a child he puts his hands over his ears.*]

SALIERI: [*Urgently, seizing his arm*]. Be merciful, therefore! Show mercy—because *we can*! That's for *us* alone to do—us, not Him!—Us! . . . Us! . . . [*Intimately*] Grant me forgiveness, Wolfgang, for pity's sake. . . . You have to! You must! You *must!*

MOZART: [*Revolting*]. NO! . . . It is *stupid!*

[*With all his strength he pushes him away.* SALIERI *staggers back.* MOZART *glares at him—and suddenly speaks, like a scared child.*]

Go away! [*He stamps his foot.*] Go away *now!* . . . Now!!

[*He makes fierce little jabs of dismissal and, when* SALIERI *does not move, defiantly shoots out his lips and emits one of his fart noises. And another, louder and more challenging. Then suddenly he snatches up his blanket and runs headlong across the room, skitters to a stop and falls to the floor, hurling the blanket over his head and holding it tight to conceal himself entirely. Under this covering he sits quite still.* SALIERI *approaches him carefully.*]

SALIERI: [*Quietly*]. Wolfgang? . . . Wolfgang? . . . Hear me, for the last time.

[*The muffled figure starts to rock slowly to and fro.* SALIERI *kneels behind him.*]

I'm begging now. On my knees. Grant me your forgiveness, won't you please?

[*Under his blanket* MOZART *starts faintly to sing his father's little bedtime "Kissing Song"—nonsense words to the tune of "Twinkle, Twinkle, Little Star!"*]

MOZART: [*Singing*]. "Oragna figata fa! Marina gamina fa!"

[*And the sound of three kisses.*]

SALIERI: Please, Wolfgang. *Ti imploro!*

[*The song comes again, in strict repetition, together with the kisses. This he now repeats again and again without stopping, a little louder and a little more desperately each time.* SALIERI *speaks with equal intensity over it.*]

For all my sins against you. All my damages, my trespasses unnumbered—absolve me now! For all my cruelties—my slanders and malice—my destructive wickedness and most unworthy deeds—absolve me now!

[*The singing has grown faster and mechanical, as if being used as a charm to keep him at bay. Above it* SALIERI *finally cries out in anguish to the impervious figure.*]

Amadeus! . . . *Mi dia l'INDULGENZA!!!!*

[*The singing stops.* SALIERI *waits, expectantly. A pause.*]

SALIERI: [*Hard*]. Do it. . . . Do it!! [*But the singing implacably resumes.*]

[*For a moment, kneeling behind him,* SALIERI *reaches out to grip* MOZART—*but cannot. He withdraws his hand, and rises instead. The singing sounds much lower.*]

SALIERI: [*To audience*]. Reduce the man—reduce the God. Behold my vow fulfilled. The profoundest voice in the world reduced to a nursery tune.

[MOZART *stops singing.*]

[*Very bitterly*] And so finally I left. Refused. Unheard! [*Looking to Heaven*] Of course! [*He is almost laughing.*] Of course! . . . [*To God*] Grazie—per sempre!!

[*He steps downstage towards the audience.*]

And never—never after—could I confess to anyone. Until I summoned You—tonight. [*Pause*] My last.

SCENE 17

[*He moves to one side.* CONSTANZE *appears upstage, bonnet in hand and wearing a shawl. She has returned from Baden. She comes downstage toward the blanketed figure on the floor.*]

CONSTANZE: [*Tentatively*]. Wolfi? . . . I'm back.

MOZART: [*Hardly daring to believe it*]. Stanzi? . . .

CONSTANZE: Yes, my love. . . . Little-husband-of-my-heart!

MOZART: Oh!

[*She bends down and helps him to his feet. He is very frail now—they embrace, he clinging to her in overwhelming pleasure.*]

CONSTANZE: I'm sorry. I'm sorry. I'm sorry . . .

[MOZART *gives a groan.*]

Oh—my dear. . . . Come now—come with me. . . . Come on, now. There . . . There . . .

[MOZART *sits weakly.*]

MOZART: [*Like a child still, and most earnestly*]. Salieri . . . Salieri has killed me.

CONSTANZE: [*Indulgently*]. Yes, my dear.

[*Practically she busies herself clearing the table of its manuscripts, its candle, its bottles and its inkwell.*]

MOZART: He has! He told me so.

CONSTANZE: Yes, yes: I'm sure.

[*She finds the chair cushions and places them at the head of the table.*]

MOZART: [*Petulantly*]. He did . . . He did!

CONSTANZE: Hush now, lovey.

[*She helps her dying husband onto the table, now his bed. He lies down, and she covers him with her shawl.*]

I'm back to take care of you. I'm here now for always!

MOZART: [*In distress*]. Salieri. . . . Salieri. . . .

[*He starts to weep.*]

CONSTANZE: Oh lovey, be silent now. No one has hurt you. You'll get better soon, I promise.

[*The* VENTICELLI *steal in to* SALIERI.]

V.1: [*Quietly*]. Dr. Closset says there's little hope.

V.2: No point in seeing him at all.

V.1 & V.2: [*Together*]. Especially as he cannot pay.

V.1: They say he's still trying to finish that Mass.

V.2: But little wife won't let him anymore!

[*The* VENTICELLI *leave. Faintly the Lacrimosa of the Requiem Mass begins to sound.* MOZART *sits up to hear it—leaning against his wife's shoulders. His hand begins feebly to beat out drum measures from the music. During the whole of the following it is evident that he is composing the Mass in his head, and does not hear his wife at all.*]

CONSTANZE: Can you hear me? Try to, Wolferl . . . Wolfi-polfi. . . . Try to hear. If I've been a bore—if I've nagged a bit about money, it didn't mean anything. It's only because I'm spoilt. You spoilt me, lovey. You've got to get well, Wolfi—because we need you. Karl and Baby Franz as well. There's only the three of us: we don't cost much. Just don't leave us—we wouldn't know what to do without you. And you wouldn't know much either, up in Heaven, without us. You soppy thing. You can't even cut up your own meat without help! . . . I'm not clever, lovey. It can't have been easy living with a goose. But I've looked after you, you must admit that. And I've given you fun too—quite a lot, really! . . . Are you listening?

[MOZART'*s drum strokes get slower, and stop.*]

Know one thing. It was the best day of my life when you married me. And as long as I live I'll be the most honored woman in the world. . . . *Can you hear me?*

[*She becomes aware that* MOZART *is dead. She opens her mouth in a silent scream, raising her arm in a rigid gesture of grief. The great chord of the "Amen" does not resolve itself, but lingers on in intense reverberation.*]

SCENE 18

[*The* CITIZENS OF VIENNA *enter, dressed in black.* CONSTANZE *kneels and freezes in grief as* SERVANTS *come in and stand at the four corners of the table on which the body lies.* VAN SWIETEN *also enters.*]

SALIERI: [*Hard*]. The Death Certificate said kidney failure, hastened by explosure to cold. Generous Lord Fugue paid for a pauper's funeral. Twenty other corpses. An unmarked lime pit.

[VAN SWIETEN *approaches* CONSTANZE.]

VAN SWIETEN: What I can spare, you shall have for the children. There's no need to waste it on vain show.

[*The* SERVANTS *lift the table and bear it with its burden upstage, to the Light Box, in which a cemetery appears, in stormy light.*]

SALIERI: What did I feel? . . . Pity! Pity—at last!—for the man I helped to destroy. I felt the pity my God can never feel! . . . I weakened God's flute to a thinness. God blew—as He must—without cease. The flute split in the mouth of His insatiable *need!*

[*Some of the* CITIZENS *kneel, and the* SERVANTS *swiftly tip the table:* MOZART's *body slides down into a pit at the back. We hear the sound of crows cawing and flapping up. The light goes out in the cemetery. The* CITIZENS *rise in the dark and face the back.*

[CONSTANZE *unfreezes and starts assiduously collecting the manuscripts scattered all over the floor.* SALIERI *now speaks with an increasingly aging voice: a sound soured more and more with its owner's bitterness.*]

As for Constanze, in the fullness of time she married again—a Danish diplomat, as dull as a clock—and retired to Salzburg, birthplace of the Great Composer, to become the pious keeper of his shrine.

[CONSTANZE *rises, wrapping her shawl about her, and clasping manuscripts to her bosom.*]

CONSTANZE: [*Reverentially*]. A sweeter-tongued man never lived. In ten years of blissful marriage I never heard him utter a single coarse or conceited word. The purity of his life is reflected absolutely in the purity of his music! [*More briskly*] In selling his manuscripts I charge by the ink. So many notes, so many schillings. . . . That seems to me the simplest way.

[*She leaves the stage, a pillar of rectitude.*]

SALIERI: One amazing fact emerged concerning that mysterious Messenger with the skeletal face and the [*Imitating it*] sinister rasping voice, who came to commission the Requiem. Mozart had not imagined him. He was *real!* . . . The man was the weird-looking Servant of an eccentric Nobleman, who longed to write music and be praised for it. His wife had just died, so he sent this Servant in deepest secrecy to order a Mass from Mozart. Incredibly the Nobleman's plan was actually to copy out the manuscript himself—and pass it off as his own work! [*Pause*] It would seem there is literally nothing a man won't stoop to in order to be thought a great composer!

[*The lights come up. The* CITIZENS *turn around and advance on* SALIERI, *bowing to him, and kissing their hands extravagantly. During his following speech they all fall on their knees in an adoring ring around him, clapping their hands at him with silent vigor and relentlessly extending their arms upwards and upwards, until they seem to obliterate him.*]

And so I stayed on in the City of Musicians, reverenced by all:
On and on and on for *thirty-two years*. And slowly I came to
understand the nature of God's punishment. [*Demanding
directly of the audience*] What had I asked for in that church as
a boy? Was it not *fame*? Well now I had it! I was to become,
quite simply, the most famous musician in Europe! . . . I was to
be bricked up in fame! Buried in fame! Embalmed in fame! . . .
This was my sentence—I must endure thirty-two years of being
called "distinguished" by people incapable of distinguishing!
And finally—when my nose had been rubbed in fame to vomit-
ing—Receptions, Awards, Civic Medals, and Chains—suddenly,
his masterstroke!

[*The* CITIZENS *freeze.*]

It would all be taken away from me—every scrap.

> [*The* CITIZENS *rise, turn away from him and walk indiffer-
> ently off stage. The Finale of the Jupiter Symphony is heard,
> swelling louder.*]

[SALIERI's *voice over music*] Mozart's music would sound everywhere—and mine in place on earth. I must survive to see myself
become . . . *extinct.* . . . [*Calling up savagely*] Nemico dei
Nemici! Dio implacabile!

> [*The curtains of the Light Box close. A* SERVANT *brings on
> the wheelchair and places it centrally, as before. Another* SER-
> VANT *brings on the old dressing gown, shawl and turban.*
> SALIERI *divests himself of his wig and cloak and puts on these
> former clothes, once more becoming the old man. He sits in
> the wheelchair.*
> *The lights change. Six o'clock strikes. The* SERVANTS *leave,
> taking the wig, cloak and hat.*]

SCENE 19

Salieri's Apartment, November 1823

SALIERI: [*To audience*]. Dawn has come. I must release you. One moment's violence and it is over. You see, I cannot accept this. To be sucked into oblivion—not even my name remembered. Oh no: I did not live on earth to be His joke for eternity. I have one trick left me—see how He deals with this!

[*Confidentially*] All this week I have been shouting out about murder. You heard me yourselves—do you remember? "Mozart—*pietà!* Pardon your assassin! Mozart!"

[*Whispers of "*SALIERI*" begin: at first faintly, as at the start of the play. During the following they grow in volume, in strict and operatic counterpoint to* SALIERI'*s speeches.*]

WHISPERERS: [*Faintly*]. *Salieri!* . . .

SALIERI: [*Triumphantly*]. I did this deliberately! . . . My servants carried the news into the street!

WHISPERERS: [*Louder*]. *Salieri!*

SALIERI: The streets repeated it to one another!

WHISPERERS: [*Louder*]. *Salieri!* . . . *Salieri!* . . .

SALIERI: Now my name is on every tongue! Vienna, City of Scandals, has a scandal worthy of it at last!

WHISPERERS: *SALIERI!* . . . *ASSASSIN!* . . . *ASSASSIN!* . . . *SALIERI!*

SALIERI: [*Falsetto, enjoying it*]. "Can it be true? . . . Is it possible? . . . Did he do it after all? . . ."

WHISPERERS: [*Fortissimo*]. *SALIERI!*

SALIERI: Well, my friends, now they all know for sure! They will learn of my dreadful death—and they will believe the lie forever! After today, whenever men speak of Mozart's name with love, they will speak of mine with loathing! As his name grows in the world, so will mine—if not in fame, then in infamy. I'm going to be immortal after all!—And He will be powerless to prevent that! [*He laughs harshly.*] So, *Signore*—see now if man is mocked!

[*He rises and addresses the audience simply, gently and directly.*]

Amici cari. I was born a pair of ears, and nothing else. It is only through hearing music that I know God exists. Only through writing music that I could worship. . . . All around me men hunger for General Rights. I hungered only for particular notes. They seek Liberty for Mankind. I sought only slavery for myself. To be owned—ordered—exhausted by an Absolute. This was denied me—and with it all meaning.

[*He produces a cutthroat razor from his dressing gown pocket, and carefully opens it.*]

Now I go to become a ghost myself. I will stand in the shadows when you come here to this earth in your turns. And when you feel the dreadful bite of your failures—and the taunting of an unachievable, uncaring God—I will whisper my name to you: "Antonio Salieri: Patron Saint of Mediocrities!" And in the depth of your downcastness you can pray to me. And I will forgive you. *Vi saluto.*

[*He cuts his throat, and falls backwards into the wheelchair.* MOZART's *somber Masonic Funeral Music sounds in the background.*

The COOK *enters, carrying a plate of buns for breakfast, and, seeing* SALIERI, *screams in horror. The* VALET *rushes in from the opposite side. Together they pull the wheelchair with its slumped body backwards upstage, and anchor it in midstage. And then the* VENTICELLI *appear again, in the costume of 1823.* VENTICELLO I *carries books and a newspaper.*]

V.I: Beethoven's Conversation Book, November eighteen twenty-three. Visitors write the news for the deaf man.

[*He hands a book to* VENTICELLO 2.]

V.2: [*Reading*]. "Salieri has cut his throat—but is still alive!"

[SALIERI *stirs and comes to life, sitting up and looking about him in outraged bewilderment.*

The VALET *and the* COOK *depart.* SALIERI *stares out front like an astonished gargoyle.*]

V.1: Beethoven's Conversation Book, eighteen twenty-four. Visitors write the news for the deaf man.

[*He hands another book to* VENTICELLO 2.]

V.2: [*Reading*]. "Salieri is quite deranged. He keeps claiming that he is guilty of Mozart's death, and made away with him by poison."

[*The lights narrow to a bright cone, beating on* SALIERI.]

V.1: The *German Musical Times*, May twenty-fifth, eighteen twenty-five.

[*He hands newspaper to* VENTICELLO 2.]

V.2: [*Reading*]. "Our worthy Salieri just cannot die. In the frenzy of his imagination he is even said to accuse himself of complicity in Mozart's early death. A rambling of the mind believed in truth by no one but the deluded old man himself."

[*The music stops.*]

[SALIERI *lowers his head, conceding defeat.*]

V.1: I don't believe it.

V.2: I don't believe it.

V.1: I don't believe it.

V.2: I don't believe it.

V.1 & V.2: [*Together*]. *No one believes it in the world!*

[*The* VENTICELLI *go off. The lights dim a little.* SALIERI *stirs, rises, comes down front and looks out far into the darkness of the theater.*]

SALIERI: Mediocrities everywhere—now and to come—I absolve you all. Amen!

[*He extends his arms upwards and outwards to embrace the*

assembled audience in a wide gesture of benediction—finally folding his arms high across his breast.
The lights fade to blackness, as the last four chords of the Masonic Funeral Music of Wolfgang Amadeus Mozart sound through the theater.]

END

SALIERI'S MARCH as played by both Salieri and Mozart, Mozart playing it faster, lighter, and less decoratively.

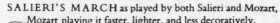

MOZART'S TRANSFORMATION PROCESS:

"That fourth doesn't quite work, does it?"

"Let's try the third above . . . . . ."   "Ah! . . . "

"NON PIU ANDRAI" arranged for piano by Kevin Leeman

At first tentatively

ABOUT THE AUTHOR

Peter Shaffer was born in Liverpool, England, in 1926. During the Second World War he worked as a conscript in a coal mine; later he studied history on a scholarship to Cambridge University, and departed thence to New York. There he worked in a Doubleday bookstore, and the Forty-second Street library, living for much of the time in Hell's Kitchen, and returning three years later to London convinced of his own unemployability. In some desperation he wrote his first play, *Five Finger Exercise*, which was produced in London in 1958 to widespread approval (in New York in 1959, where it won the Drama Critics Circle Award), thereby relieving him of the necessity of working in other stores or offices.

The success of his first play suggested to Shaffer that he might be a dramatist at heart. Partly because he had no aptitude for doing anything else, he sat down during the ensuing years and produced other plays. All of these met with great success, first in London and then in New York: *The Private Ear* and *The Public Eye*, a double bill, in 1962; *The Royal Hunt of the Sun*, an epic concerning the conquest of Peru, which the eminent English critic Bernard Levin described as "the greatest play of our generation," in 1964; and in the following year *Black Comedy*, a romp designed for Britain's National Theatre, which another London reviewer hailed as "the farce of the century." In 1973, the author wrote *Equus*, which ran for more than 1,200 performances on Broadway, and won all major New York critical awards. All three of the last-mentioned plays opened first at the National Theatre of Great Britain and were directed by John Dexter, in whom Shaffer found a brilliant colleague.

Amadeus was the fourth successful work Shaffer originated at the British National Theatre, where, directed by Sir Peter Hall, it won the Evening Standard Drama Award. It opened on Broadway in December 1980, running for well over a thousand performances, and won the Tony Award. Milos Forman's film of the play won eight Oscars, including one for Shaffer's adaptation.

Twenty years later, the play was successfully revived in both London and New York in a completely new production by the same director, with some important textual alterations. It is this version which is published here, with an introduction by Hall and a new long Preface by the author.

Subsequent plays by Peter Shaffer include *Yonadab*, set in the court of King David; *Lettice and Lovage*, written for Maggie Smith, and triumphantly acted by her in both London and New York; *The Gift of the Gorgon*, produced by the Royal Shakespeare Company, and starring Judi Dench; and *Whom Do I Have the Honour of Addressing?*, a monologue, played at the Chichester Theatre Festival.

In 1987, Peter Shaffer was created a Commander of the British Empire, and also received the Hamburg Shakespeare Prize. In 1998, he was selected to be a founding member of the illustrious Academia Europea de Yuste, in Spain.

In 2001 he received a knighthood in the New Year's Honours List.